"A must-read! Jill Austin has masterful[inspired art that is filled with hidden m, *ing with Destiny* is a portal into discovery. You will be left pondering, soaking, contemplating, dreaming, loving, warring. You will be left . . . changed!"

—**Patricia King**, president, Extreme Prophetic

"For all people with two left feet who feel they cannot dance, this book is for you! For all those romantics who cannot wait for that ultimate dance of joy with the Bridegroom, Jill's book will prepare your hearts for that special moment. I personally cannot wait! This book made me fall in love with the Lover of my soul all over again. It is a must-read."

—**Cindy Jacobs**, cofounder, Generals International

"We are presently living in perhaps the most unique generation in Church history. It is a day foreseen and spoken about by numerous prophets and patriarchs throughout history. Something has been woven into the spiritual DNA of a body of people who are being awakened as warriors and champions. The apostle Paul emphasized that the Lord Jesus paid the price to save us and also provided a holy calling and a sacred destiny. Jill Austin's book *Dancing with Destiny* is a clarion call to this reality. Significant insight will be gained as each reader draws from this well of spiritual understanding provided through Jill's years of friendship with the Lord and her ministry experience."

—**Paul Keith Davis**, founder, WhiteDove Ministries

"Jill Austin is a mystical child of God who sees Him in a peculiar way. She is able to relate what she sees to give the normal mind a better picture of God's creative power and ability. She is a lover, and she knows how to express His love in a tangible, embraceable manner. *Dancing with Destiny* causes us to embrace God and reject all our fears, shame and regrets. Jill moves from the love of God and brings the reader of this book into the war of love. This is a captivating read for anyone."

—**Chuck D. Pierce**, president,
Glory of Zion International Ministries

"*Dancing with Destiny* is not just a book; it's a manual to help you unlock the secrets of your own destiny. It contains revelations that will empower you to be who you were created to be. Jill Austin is a master storyteller who takes real-life stories, combines them with biblical insight and proves that no matter what your circumstances may be, your destiny is in the middle of them. *Dancing with Destiny* shows that healing, salvation and miracles are part of *your* destiny. A great read!"

—**Wesley** and **Stacey Campbell**, cofounders,
Revival Now! Ministries

"We are created so our lives will have a lasting, relevant and significant impact; but only that which is truly significant comes from God. The revelation of God's destiny for our lives is a vast subject, yet Jill Austin has captured the heart of God in her book. My prayer is that God will open the eyes of your heart and bring a renewed confidence and clarity to your life in Jesus. Jill gives a fresh, creative perspective to God's calling for us to dream His dreams, to love the Bridegroom King passionately and to be one of His warring champions for Kingdom purposes. By the time you read the final page, I pray that your heart will be stirred with a fiery new passion to dance your destiny with Him!"

—**Mike Bickle**, ministry director, Friends of the Bridegroom; International House of Prayer

"The 'dreamer keys' Jill Austin presents in this book will unlock doors of hope, release a celebration of life, renew vision and fan the flames of passion in your heart as you press beyond all spiritual battles into the destiny to which you have been called. Even more, she weaves the tapestry of themes and words with her characteristic artistic craftsmanship intermingled with her passion for Jesus, the Bridegroom King."

—**Barbara J. Yoder**, senior pastor, Shekinah Christian Church; author; apostle, Breakthrough Apostolic Ministries Network; apostolic leader of Michigan and National Apostolic Council member; Global Apostolic Prayer Network

"Jill Austin has authored a very well-written and powerful book that will inspire and awaken your destiny in God. This book is like no other book. She combines her prophetic gifts with her supernatural encounters to inspire you to dream, love and war for the advancement of God's Kingdom."

—**Ché Ahn**, senior pastor, Harvest Rock Church, Pasadena

"Jill has given us a fascinating and challenging book. After reading it, we no longer want to hide behind excuses but eagerly desire for God to awaken His dreams in us. Her personal illustrations are so well presented—intriguing!"

—**Quin Sherrer**, co-author, *Lord, I Need Your Healing Power*

"I have known Jill Austin for several years and have ministered with her in this nation and in other nations. I believe she is a gift to the Body of Christ and has been given a gift of creativity, especially in her writing. Her latest book is a source of encouragement to Christians to enter into their destiny. I believe *Dancing with Destiny* will bless many."

—**Randy Clark**, founder, Global Awakening

"Jill Austin has been a longtime friend. But even before she knew me and I knew her, I saw her as a major prophetic forerunner. I would sit anonymously in her ministry meetings, saying to myself, 'Wow!' Needless to say, when a pioneer such as Jill Austin speaks or writes, I *listen*—and so should you!"

—**Steve Shultz**, The Elijah List, www.elijahlist.com

"*Dancing with Destiny* is surprising, bracing and refreshing, and it takes us into the presence of God. Jill's prophetic message and journey are anchored in the Word of God and bring wonderful and helpful illumination from the Scriptures. God's heart for a last-days generation of prophetic warriors, intercessors and artists beats loudly throughout this book. Jill lights a fire for the final harvest. Read this book! God may use it to set you ablaze."

—**Avner Boskey**, Final Frontier Ministries, Beersheva, Israel

"Read this book with the intent of entering into a more intimate, personal relationship with God than you have ever experienced. Only those who have it can impart it, and Jill Austin walks in an intimacy with God that few ever find."

—from the foreword by **Dutch Sheets**, senior pastor, Springs Harvest Fellowship, Colorado Springs

"Jill Austin has once again tapped into the heart of the Father. This book will be used to awaken the Church to dream the dreams that alter the course of world history, while putting us back on track to discover the beauty of warfare born out of intimacy with God."

—**Bill Johnson**, author, *When Heaven Invades Earth*; senior pastor, Bethel Church, Redding, Calif.

"You will soar on the winds of destiny and be caught up into the realities of the eternal as you read the pages of this inspiring book. Jill Austin is an artist, a prophetess and a stateswoman for Jesus in this generation. You will be captivated by the love of God as your soul mounts up with the wings of an eagle and you find the purpose and reason for which you were created."

—**Dr. James W.** and **Michal Ann Goll**, cofounders, Encounters Network

"Jill's book *Dancing with Destiny* awakened my heart to dream even more the glorious dreams of God. I was undone by some of the stories. They caused me to pray and press in for an even more radical walk of love. This book will delight your heart."

—**Dr. Heidi Baker**, founding director, Iris Ministries

"If you have become weary, disillusioned or discouraged in the midst of your battles, Jill Austin's new book will offer you fresh vision, new hope and obtainable keys to help unlock your destiny in places where you have felt stuck. In her engaging style, Jill will challenge you 'to dream, to love, to war'!"

—**Jane Hansen**, president/CEO, Aglow International

"Be prepared to have your brain stretched beyond your comfort zone. If you allow this to happen, then you will move into a new view of your Christian faith that will reinvigorate your understanding of the destiny the Lord has for you."

—**Paul L. Cox**, Aslan's Place

"Jill Austin is a passionate lover of Jesus. *Dancing with Destiny* will lead you into deeper intimacy and passion for the Lord as your love for Jesus intensifies. You will find open heavens and experience His presence. You will begin to dream again and believe once again that the Lord will give you the desires of your heart. As you turn the pages of this book, you will hear the voice of the Bridegroom, your warrior King, calling you, equipping you and empowering you for spiritual warfare. As the Holy Spirit unlocks chains that have kept you from moving forward to fulfill His plans and purposes in your life as a lover, a dreamer and a warrior, you will find yourself on the dance floor of eternity in the sweet embrace of the Bridegroom, and you will be dancing with destiny."

—**David Ruleman**, vice president, general manager, WAVA, Washington, D.C.

"*Dancing with Destiny* is a delight. We are in a major transition, and Jill Austin is a catalyst for this time of change. This book will help everyone realize that God is calling all of us to learn how to 'dance' with Jesus to see radical change and revolution. Just as in the 1960s and '70s, when God poured out His Spirit during the Jesus movement, we are on the verge of a much greater wave. *Dancing with Destiny* not only helps you define your purpose, but it also gives you the weapons for the battle. God is raising up the Daniels, Davids, Esthers and Deborahs to awaken us to love and take our places in the battle. This book has a warrior's call to awaken your heart to dream, to love and to war."

—**Meri Crouley**, president, Meri Crouley Ministries, *Now Is the Time* television program, Youthwave Explosion Foundation

Dancing with
DESTINY

AWAKEN YOUR HEART
TO DREAM, TO LOVE, TO WAR

JILL AUSTIN

Chosen
Grand Rapids, Michigan

Published by Chosen Books
A division of Baker Publishing Group
P.O. Box 6287, Grand Rapids, MI 49516–6287
www.chosenbooks.com

Printed in the United States of America

Library of Congress Cataloging-in-Publication Data
Austin, Jill, 1948–
    Dancing with destiny : awaken your heart to dream, to love, to war /
Jill Austin.
        p.   cm.
    ISBN 10: 0-8007-9425-7 (pbk.)
    ISBN 978-0-8007-9425-5 (pbk.)
    1. Vocation—Christianity. 2. Spirituality. I. Title.
BV4740.A97 2007
248.4—dc22   2006039229

Contents

Dedication

How do I say thank you to my very best friend, the Holy Spirit? Oh, how I love His violent love and insatiable fervency to bring suffering humanity to Jesus! I am in awe that I can partner with Him in bringing in the harvest.

He fills the lonely places of my soul as His wind blows this traveling vagabond across this terrestrial globe. Always with me, He is my confidant, counselor and strategist. His tender companionship and guidance always point to the glorious Son, Jesus.

It is as though He is standing right next to me, whispering prophetic words and revelations that proclaim destiny and birthright to many. He shows me insight into the Word and gives me glimpses into eternity. He makes me homesick to be with Him forever.

Our relationship has not been meek and mild, however! The Holy Spirit is a wild, heavenly tornado who wreaks havoc, shaking everything that can be shaken. At times He is like the roaring wind or consuming fire, but at other times He is like the gentle dove.

He is not afraid of controversy. Fear of man? He never has to deal with it; I do, though, after He has offended many. But talking and wrestling with Him into the night, I always see His great love and wisdom in challenging people to run for their highest callings.

This wondrous Person, who is God, is also an intimate friend. His colorful personality captivates my heart. My comprehension of Him has deepened over the years, forever growing. Amazing grace; that is what He gives me.

Foreword

I love considering the subject of destiny. I enjoy reading about it, studying it, even simply musing over the concept in my devotional time. It awakens my heart to the fact that our Creator is a God of purpose and design, always beginning with the end in mind. Isaiah 46:10, one of my favorite verses, actually says He "[declares] the end from the beginning" (NASB). I have preached from this passage several times and think on it often, and yet I am still filled with wonder each time it comes to mind.

Just when I believe I have mined all the gold from this mother lode of truth, Jill Austin slaps me upside the head (that's Texan for "shocks me") with the phrase *dancing with destiny*. My response went something like this:

Whoa! Slow down. My mind is saying, "No match found."

Where did that come from?

Where does she get this stuff?

I cannot wait to read this book!

I have known Jill long enough now that nothing she says should surprise me, but this one overloaded my circuits temporarily. Then my carnal side engaged in the discussion and I found myself thinking, *I wish I had said that!* (As you have probably discerned, that would have been difficult given my mind's reaction to simply hearing it.) Oh well, at least I made it into the foreword!

Do we really have a destiny from God? Absolutely. And though He has chosen not to share all of it with us up front—the Hebrew word *achariyth* conveys the concept of backing into the future, like a person rowing a boat—rest assured God has wonderful plans for you, plans for good, not evil (see Jeremiah 29:11).

The New Testament Greek word for "destiny," *proorizo*, is filled with hope. The root, *horizo*, gives us our word *horizon*; the prefix means "in advance." God has planned a future for us, determining our horizons before we were ever born (see Psalm 139:13–16). This does not mean everything that occurs in our lives is preplanned by God; He does not cause us to sin, fail or experience devastation just so He can give us a testimony. But it does mean He has a finish line in mind for us and a preordained way of recovery when forces try to derail us.

In this great book, Jill marries two enigmatic pieces of our destiny: *worshiping* and *warring*. She calls our dance with destiny "the dance of a warrior." "You are not just a dreamer and lover," she declares. "You are a warrior!"

She is right—we have become the enigma. We are "the generation of those who seek Him, who seek Your face" (Psalm 24:6) and also those who declare that our God is "the LORD strong and mighty, the LORD mighty in battle" (verse 8). We are worshiping warriors, loving liberators. Though some in the world try to brand Christians as radicals who want control of everything, we know we are really freedom fighters on a mission of mercy.

Read this book with the intent of entering into a more intimate, personal relationship with God than you have ever experienced. Only those who have it can impart it, and Jill Austin walks in an intimacy with God that few ever find.

And read it with the intent that you will become a greater warrior—one of God's "bravehearts." You were made for war. He did not intend for you to sit by while others won the victor's crown. God has made you more than a conqueror!

Don't wait another day. Ask your heavenly Father to impart His heart to you through this book; He desperately wants to do so. He is ready to dance. *Are you?*

Dutch Sheets, senior pastor,
Springs Harvest Fellowship, Colorado Springs

Preface

The Invitation

> You shall no longer be termed Forsaken, nor shall your land any more be termed Desolate; but you shall be called Hephzibah, and your land Beulah; for the Lord delights in you, and your land shall be married. For as a young man marries a virgin, so shall your sons marry you; and as the bridegroom rejoices over the bride, so shall your God rejoice over you.
>
> Isaiah 62:4–5

The most breathtaking moment in a wedding is when the bride glides down the aisle, wrapped in the most glorious garment imaginable. Crowds are hushed and all eyes are fixed on her for she has captured the room, just by her appearance. The couple's passion changes the atmosphere as the wedding guests catch intimate gazes between the two lovers. Hearts soften; old dreams and

promises are quickened; hope is renewed. An ancient longing to be loved is awakened again.

The mystery of the Gospel is the mystery of a divine,
eternal love story between the Bridegroom and the Bride.
God is calling for His Bride—for you. He is longing for
you to know Him more intimately through the prophetic
journey of your life.

This is not an ordinary adventure, any more than the
first dance of a newly married couple is an ordinary dance.
It is a dance with *destiny*. Just as the couple steps onto the
ballroom floor to begin their new life together, learning to
waltz as one, so you are called to step into the journey of
a lifetime with your Bridegroom King.

I love the waltz. It is beautiful and romantic. It begins
with a simple three-part box step and feels comfortable,
effortless and familiar. The music is hypnotically smooth.
It is the dance that draws guests onto the floor alongside
the happy couple and into sweet embraces of their own.

In time the band takes a break and the wedding crowd
begins to mingle. When the band returns, the music has a
different cadence. The rhythm has an exciting pounding
beat. The wedding guests stand at the edge of the dance
floor. Nobody knows quite what to do! You wait.

The Bridegroom King walks out to the center of the ballroom floor looking magnificent. The fresh fire of burning
love is in His eyes. He turns and extends His hand—toward
you. You flush with joy at such a display of affection. In His
hand is a long-stemmed red rose, and He offers it to you
with an invitation. Joyfully He says, "Let's tango!"

Dancing is the epitome of partnership. It involves respect,
dignity and strength. It takes courage to follow your heart
and to let your inhibitions go. It shows who is willing to be
vulnerable and grow as a partner and who is not.

Will you take His hand and dance all night? Or will you
stand aloof and watch others grow in their journeys?

It is risky. You know you could look foolish. The tango moves outside of the box. It is passionate—perhaps too intimate. But you are willing to believe that the Bridegroom King knows the steps. You find that you long to be in His arms. You say yes and accept the red rose. You take His hand and begin to move across the ballroom floor.

As you share the intimacy of the dance with Him, you find that He is utterly wild yet utterly safe at the same time. He knows your dreams! He wants to share them with you. He wants you to know love such as you have never known. And as you find the freedom to dream and love, you discover something else.

You lean more closely into Him to listen, your feet moving with His in time with the staccato music, and you realize that you can hear His heart beating. At first you recognize the sounds of an orchestra—flowing strings and blaring brass—but then you hear in the distance the music of different tribes and peoples. There is an insistent beating of drums, the sound of war in the nations—and in your own backyard. You are not just a dreamer and lover, you are a warrior! You are meant to bring the councils of heaven down to earth.

It becomes the dance of a warrior, something like King David's dance when the Ark of the Covenant was being returned to Jerusalem. He was not worried about being dignified. He was a warrior celebrating victory, and he displayed his joy with leaping and ecstatic whirling. The Bible tells us that his wife Michal, however, watched with judgmental eyes. She was not willing to give herself to such love and abandonment of her principles. And what happened? David's exuberance pleased the Lord, and Michal's critical heart led to the loss of her destiny. She, who could have borne kings, was forever barren.

What about you? If you have even a glimmer of belief in yourself and in your journey with the Lord, then you have what it takes to dance with your destiny. This master dancer—the dreamer God and Creator of the universe—moves with beauty, grace and skill. He transforms your life as He takes you from the tango to jazz to ballet to the rumba. Your heart becomes alive with anticipation, joy and adventure.

It is a fascinating journey. He is so fun and full of life, you want more of Him. You love the partnership of the Bride with the Bridegroom King. Catching just one glimpse of His eye gives you the courage to follow your heart. You also realize that greater intimacy with Him makes a way for you to testify of His great love to a hurt and dying world.

Gradually the music returns to a fluid and graceful waltz. He draws you close and whispers, "Come with Me, My beloved. Your destiny, your journey, will surpass your wildest dreams if you follow Me."

Will you stay close to His heart and learn to dream, to love and to war? Will you let Him show you the steps of your journey?

Will you dance with destiny?

Acknowledgments

This book started with a dream of being awakened to the radical adventures of partnering with God. After returning from a grueling around-the-world ministry trip to Africa and then Korea, my copartner in ministry, Linda Valen, and I found ourselves recuperating on the beaches of Hawaii with our dear friends Scott and Vicky Vanderhoof. He is a surfboard shaper and land developer; she is an intercessor and one of those people who do all things well. They are unique entrepreneurs, yet they know how to rest, play and enjoy being fully alive. They lived what I was going to write about—the fact that dreamers and lovers make better warriors.

Deep heartfelt fellowship and sharing the vision for the book stirred fresh revelation. While swimming with sea turtles, watching the surfers catch mountainous waves, soaking in the sun, picnicking on the beach, enjoying beautiful sunsets and taking naps during the day, we heard the Lord say to us, *Your dreams are like a cup of water, but My dreams for you are like the vastness of an ocean.*

It was a journey into uncharted waters that ambushed all of us as the Lord assembled His "dream team."

Linda has served with me for more than twelve years. She is an armor bearer and warrior for the cause of Jesus. She helped to strategize concepts for the book, giving language to our brainstorming times and putting things in order with such revelation and heart. I call her "my valentine." This book would not have been possible without her tenacity to work extreme hours with me to give birth to this "baby."

Cathy Arkle, a revelatory and creative visionary, also became a part of this prophetic adventure. I often called her the "Peter Pan" of the group! She brought childlikeness to our brainstorming sessions as well as great wisdom. As an artist, she brought a palette of colors that splashed all over the canvas of the book. We spent many a session burning the midnight oil.

David and Tracy Ruleman and Rich and Pam Boyer have been marvelous comrades and intercessors for more than thirty years. They have stood with me through amazing "God adventures" and glorious mountaintop experiences. They love the glory and the presence of God and are lifelong friends whom I love.

Karen Hol, a gifted artist and writer, is truly a sister in the Lord and a confidant in the ministry, cheering me on with her voice of counsel and wisdom. She has been a faithful and loyal friend for more than thirty years, as well.

The foundational portion of this "dream team" could not have happened without the excellence and dedication of Jane Campbell, editorial director of Chosen Books. She had such vision for this project. A lover of the Word and the Spirit, Jane is a woman of integrity who is a visionary and gatekeeper, bridging the publisher with the authors and the masses.

Ann Weinheimer was another significant member of my "dream team" whom the Lord brought into this exciting journey. Ann's joy and enthusiasm, along with her gifting as a wordsmith, significantly molded this book. What a delight she was to work with! Her suggestions and revelation helped to fashion the creativity of the dance in this book.

Chosen Books staff, you have outdone yourselves! Thank you for helping to birth such a unique book. Your exceptionally creative team really went the extra mile. You are awesome.

I want to thank all the staff, intercessors, friends and partners of Master Potter Ministries who have helped me on this prophetic journey. I felt your prayers and your love. What incredible sacrifices everyone has made to launch another book!

A very special thank you goes to my sisters, Judith Peterson and Joan McMaster, whose gifts of wisdom and insight have continually cheered me on and challenged me to dream big dreams. Jon Austin, my brother, has been a source of joy with his childlike heart and love for Jesus during this project.

Introduction

Has your life turned out totally different from the way you dreamed it would be? Have you grown weary because of shattered hopes, delayed answers and painful regrets? Perhaps you have gone through the routines of life and walked with God for a long time, but now you seem to have lost vision for your life. Once when you were young and vibrant in God, you had a cause to die for, but instead of dying for a cause, now you find yourself dying.

Can you remember a time in your life when you were doing something that really made you excited to get out of bed each day? When you felt fully alive? Those were times that you *knew* you were walking in your gifting and destiny, and you felt the pleasure of God. You were invigorated and excited about your life. But then reality hits and you say to yourself, *I am tired of hearing about the word* destiny *because that is not what is happening in my life.* You begin to wonder if your life has any eternal value or meaning.

But what if *destiny* was defined differently? What if it was not anything we thought it was?

Destiny in Motion

Think with me for a moment. Destiny is a progression of cycles and seasons. It happens over time, spanning the decades of your life. Destiny is like a giant tapestry—maybe twelve miles high, twelve miles wide and twelve miles deep. It is multileveled and, even more, it is organic and ever changing. Your destiny is a fascinating and complex weaving that came from the very heart of Jesus.

It is true. It may be too amazing for the heart or mind even to grasp, but you started in the imagination of God. He has *already* dreamed about you. Your destiny is the divine journey that you are living *right now*. It may look different from what you imagined, but God, the masterful dream weaver, does not make mistakes with anyone's life and destiny.

> For You did form my inward parts; You did knit me together in my mother's womb. I will confess and praise You for You are fearful and wonderful and for the awful wonder of my birth! Wonderful are Your works, and that my inner self knows right well. My frame was not hidden from You when I was being formed in secret [and] intricately and curiously wrought [as if embroidered with various colors] in the depths of the earth [a region of darkness and mystery]. Your eyes saw my unformed substance, and in Your book all the days [of my life] were written before ever they took shape, when as yet there was none of them.
>
> Psalm 139:13–16, AMPLIFIED

My desire is to awaken your heart to new adventures so that you are fully alive in God. I believe that you will receive fresh revelation about the process of dancing with your destiny. It involves transforming your mind so you see your life through the heart of God instead of through your circumstances.

This book offers different keys to unlock the door of hope and celebrate your life. The dreamer key will give you renewed vision for your journey. The lover key will ignite your heart with fresh passion. And the warrior key will release strategies and blueprints for the spiritual battles you will face.

Wild Like the Sea

There is a certain wildness about dreaming impossible dreams, but God wants to fulfill the desires of your heart. He wants you to imagine the unimaginable, and then He will take you even farther. You cannot go backward—you know too much. Where would you go anyway? There is a longing in you that can be satisfied only by God Himself. This knowledge is what keeps you sharp and on the cutting edge spiritually.

I live on the West Coast, and when I think of wildness, I often think of the sea. It can change in a second from gently lapping waves to dangerous riptides, or from raging storms to peaceful settings for the sun to slip into at night.

Have you ever ridden a wave runner? For those who are landlocked, this is a "motorcycle" that you ride on water. Whenever I can, I rent one and take it outside the harbor into the wild seas—up over big waves and down into deep swells. At times it is scary to be so adventuresome, but it is also exhilarating.

There is yet another way of looking at destiny! Surfing the big waves can be frightening. It often means leaving our comfort zones. You might have been wooed out into the surf in the past only to come back with bruised bones, cracked ribs, a concussion and strained muscles. Disillusioned, you have settled for sitting on the beach and watching others ride the waves.

But if we sit and wait for that big dream called "destiny" simply to show up like a tidal wave one day, we are likely to be even more disappointed. Destiny is not something

25

in the future, something that we will attain at the end of life. If we wait forever to seek our dreams, we will never find them.

Will you start to dream again? Will you join me? We can do this together. Perhaps it is time for you to snorkel, to hop on a jet ski or even to catch a big wave on a surfboard.

Surfers know about adventure. They travel the world following their dream of flowing in harmony with something more powerful than they are. They are in love with the thrill of being challenged. They go into the surf knowing that the pounding pressure of the mountainous waves could kill them. Big wave surfers understand living in the moment.

Why do people do things like that? *Because when you have something big enough to die for, you become fully alive.* It is in the heart of every person to have a cause, a desire for radical adventures that challenge the very core of our being. There needs to be a cry in us that says, "I want to have a cause! I want to have an awakening that is big enough to dream about, fall in love with and die for."

If you are part of the Body of Christ, you have a cause: The Lord's heart aches for the lost. And the amazing thing is that your own personal dreams, your journey, can be interwoven with God's great battle plans being "strategized" right now in the heavenlies. The battle may take place on different fronts—in the nations, in your relationships, even in your thoughts. But that is part of the thrill.

The Bible tells us that Jesus spoke to someone who was, in every respect, dead to his dreams. Delayed answers and shattered hopes had left him with no seeming possibility of fulfilling his destiny.

Are you in that situation? Then listen to Jesus' words: "Lazarus, come forth!"

The Lord is calling you to come forth, take off the grave clothes and put on your surfing shorts.

Join me. It is time for the adventures to begin.

Part One

DREAMERS

May He grant you according to your heart's desire, and fulfill all your purpose.

Psalm 20:4

1

In the Broom Closet of Prayer

I ran out of my pastor's office, absolutely terrified. *I've got to find a place to hide so I can hear from God.* At the end of the hall a door caught my eye. In desperation I rushed to it, ducked inside the tiny dark room and closed the door behind me. The room smelled of industrial strength disinfectant; I could feel the long handles of brooms and mops. My heart was pounding. I knew I had heard a Scripture once about getting into a prayer closet, so I whispered, "Okay, God, I'm listening. Quick! Help!"

What am I doing? I can't believe I'm hiding in the closet. I cried out again, "Lord, I've got to go out any minute and talk in front of two thousand people. I need a script. I didn't understand I needed a script. Lord, I need to hear from You." I was close to panic. I laid my head against the mops and brooms, breathing the dust and fumes from the cleaning products, as I continued crying out to the Lord. In just a few moments I would have to step up onto the platform at our church's popular Saturday night service and minister for the first time in my life. Sweat dripped down my face.

"Lord, I'm listening. What do You want to say?" I strained to listen but I heard nothing. "Lord, are You going to talk to me?" Nothing.

Have you noticed that the harder you keep trying to hear Him, the more you seem to get spiritually constipated? It seems that nothing comes out.

All of a sudden I realized that my pastor was probably wondering where I was. *I'd better get out. It wouldn't be cool for people to find me hiding in a closet.* "Okay, Lord, when the coast is clear I'm going to step out of this closet and walk back to his office, and no one will even know that I've been hiding here."

With my ear to the door I heard my pastor ask, "Has anyone seen her? It's time to start."

One of the leather-clad musicians said, "She's down the hallway in the closet."

I then began pleading with God to rapture me! I could hear heavy footsteps coming toward me. I was trapped. All I could think was, *Can I just vanish? Can the earth open up and swallow me? What can I do? How did I get stuck here in this closet? I'm an artist; I'm a potter. I don't belong on a stage. Why did I agree to talk to an audience while seated at my potter's wheel? I obviously didn't understand what I was getting into.*

The predicament I now faced had started just five days earlier. This was 1971, and I was a hippie who came back to the Lord during the Jesus People movement. I had driven my funky broken-down van over the mountains to a Christian arts festival in Washington State. Great crowds of people from a five-state area had come to hear musicians and speakers, watch dramas and purchase crafts from artisans selling leather, jewelry, blown glass and pottery. We artisans were relegated to the lower field, a place of significantly less prominence than the performing artists' and speakers' platforms.

I loved Jesus passionately, but I was struggling with a few things: I was still trying, for instance, to give up profanity and my two-pack-a-day cigarette habit. But in spite of my brokenness I really wanted to serve Him, and I wanted Him to do something with my life.

So I came to the Christian arts festival, set up a display booth with my potter's wheel and sat on the field and made vessels, but no one paid much attention. "You know, Lord," I told Him as the days passed, "if there isn't any life in this, then I don't want to do it. I don't want to be chained to the god of art."

I had just received my bachelor of fine arts degree and a secondary-education teaching degree from the University of Puget Sound in Tacoma, Washington. As a studio artist—a production potter—I had made thousands of pieces of pottery and had won many awards. I was at the top of my game. But after coming to Jesus I had grown restless; there had to be more to my life than just making pots. My heart ached for more of Him; I was in one of those destiny-seeking, uncomfortable transition times.

"Lord," I would pray, "I want You to use my life. What can I do? I see how You use the musicians, but I can't play an instrument. You use singers, but I can't sing. You use the pastors, but I'm not called to do that. I know You use people in the church nursery, but I'm not sure which end is up as far as kids. How can You use me? I'm just a mudslinger."

Then in the busyness of the festival, I resolved something in my heart. "Lord," I said, "I am going to fast and pray for the next three days, until the last day of the festival. I don't ever want to do pottery again unless somehow I can hear Your voice in this."

Not long after that prayer several children came and asked me to make them a pot. I told them that I would not be making pots again until the last day of the festival.

They said that was fine, but they kept returning to remind me of my promise.

During those next three days of fasting, the Lord led me to the words of Jeremiah 18:2–6, verses that began: "Arise and go down to the potter's house, and there I will cause you to hear My words." I was transfixed. "Wow, Lord!" I said. "There are mudslingers in the Bible. You're a potter! But, still, how can You use my life?"

The last day of the festival came. It was drizzling and cold, matching my discouragement. I was not any closer to understanding my calling than I had been three days earlier. The children arrived on schedule and found me in my pottery booth, surrounded by hundreds of pots I had made to sell. With one voice they chorused, "You promised! You promised!" I really did not want to go out in the bad weather. In my heart I was saying, *No, I lied. Can't you see that it's raining?* But I was trapped by my promise.

I took a piece of clay and with exasperation said, "Oh, all right. Come on." I stepped outside the shelter of my booth onto the muddy field where my wheel was set up. *I shouldn't have promised. This is ridiculous.* The children were practically jumping they were so excited.

Now I had to deal not only with making a pot in the rain but with my bad attitude. I was frustrated and angry, and I especially did not feel like being out in a muddy field. But I wrestled to get my heart right because I reasoned that the Lord would surely take me to the woodshed later if I was not nice to the children.

So as the rain dripped in my eyes, I plopped the lump of clay onto the potter's wheel and began to center it. Suddenly I heard the Lord's voice. It was not a big holy moment. The heavens did not open and the angels did not begin to sing. But, although I did not realize it yet, God had just ambushed me by using those little children to push me through the "birth canal" and into what would eventually become my destiny.

As I spun the wheel I heard Him say, *I will center you and take away your double-mindedness. I know you.* As my hands started to go into the foundations of the clay, He said, *I will build a foundation that is based on the Word of God. When you were in your mother's womb, I knew you and loved you.* Revelation started to flow through my whole being. My hands became His hands. He added the living Word of God to every motion.

You are beautifully and fearfully made.

I was listening to Him talk and thought, *Wow, Lord, that is really good!*

He responded, *Well, if it's that good, why don't you repeat it?*

So, still concentrating on my pot, I simply repeated what I heard. I said things like, "I know your destiny, and I know your birthright. Your form was not hidden from Me. Your name is written on the palm of My hand." As I spoke, the revelation of the Lord fell on me. A crowd started to form around me out in the rain and the dreariness. People started to laugh and cry.

As I pulled up the walls on the pot, I repeated His words: "I will shape you and pull up your walls, almost to the breaking point. But I know who you are. I know your shape; I know your form; I know your function. My fingerprints will be seen on you."

I ended up making two vessels that day, and when I got off the wheel I was trembling. I knew the Lord had given me a profound gift. I knew He had spoken through me. I did not know this was prophecy. This was the early seventies; there was no language about prophecy yet.

A few days later my pastor, Pastor Shackett from People's Church, phoned me and said he had heard that I was doing stories on the potter's wheel.

"I only did two at the festival," I explained. I knew that our church had Saturday night concerts and that they featured local talent before the main band performed. He asked if I would be willing to share my story on the wheel that next Saturday. Naively, I said I would.

When Saturday arrived, I showed up at the church with my potter's wheel, wearing my blue and white striped overalls and my clunky hiking boots. Pastor Shackett had asked me to come to his office where the musicians who would be performing that night were hanging out. They were all wearing their sleek black leather jackets and looking cool. "Hi, guys!" I said and tried to look cool, too. It was really hard, though, to project a cool image the way I was dressed.

My pastor turned to me and asked, "Do you have your script? Are you ready?"

I was taken aback. "Script? What do you mean by a script?" You see, my major was fine arts, not theater. I had never dealt with scripts.

Now *he* was taken aback. "Well," he said by way of explanation, "you have to have a script."

I felt my face beginning to flush. All the band members were looking at me. "Okay," I said. "What—what is a script?"

"I thought you were going to tell a story on your potter's wheel."

"I am."

"Well, didn't you write down your story and memorize it?" With an intense look on his face, he asked, "Haven't you done that?"

"Well, no. I didn't know I was supposed to."

"You have to have a script! What were you planning to do?"

"Well, you see," I stammered, "God, He talks to me, and I listen and then just repeat it."

He looked shocked and the words fairly erupted from him. "No! You can't do it that way!"

"You're right," I said, panic rising. "I can't do it that way."

So that is how I came to bolt from his office and run, *kalump, kalump, kalump*, down the hallway, looking desperately for a place to hear God and pray. And into the broom closet I hid, muttering, "I need a script. I need a script. I didn't know I needed a script. God, I should have asked You what I was going to talk about."

When I heard Pastor Shackett's voice in the hall, I kept hoping that the earth would open up and swallow me. Instead he knocked on the door. I responded as nonchalantly as I could, "Yes? Come in."

He pulled open the door and said sternly, "No. You come out! We're late." He towered over me. At that stage in my life I was shy and afraid of authority figures. He was a combination pastor-father figure, which added to my panic and embarrassment.

I followed him numbly to the edge of the huge stage. A few guys carried my potter's wheel for me. I bit my lip and fear gripped my heart as I watched them take it all the way to the other side. *Oh, Jesus, why did they take it over there? How am I going to go all the way across the stage?*

Pastor Shackett turned to me and said, "Let's go."

I took a step out from behind the curtain, got about ten feet onto the stage and made the mistake of looking out at the audience. I should tell you that when I had come to the church three years earlier, about two hundred people had attended. I usually took a seat in the back row, afraid even to speak to anyone. I had finally worked my way up to about the middle section. Because of the Jesus People explosion, the attendance had mushroomed and the church had built this new auditorium that held two thousand people.

So now all four thousand eyes were staring back at me. I froze. I was as motionless as the proverbial deer in the headlights. I could tell that I had a silly grin on my face, but inside I was screaming, *God, get me out of here. I promise I'll be good. I'll never sin again. I repent. Forgive me for the past, the present and the sins I haven't even committed yet.*

Why was I so stupid to say yes to this? I had no idea what I was getting myself into. I'm so totally disqualified. This was so stupid. Stupid, stupid, stupid.

I heard Pastor Shackett's voice. "Why isn't she moving?"

I thought, *I don't know. Why am I not moving?* It was as though my feet were stuck to the floor. As I continued to look at the crowd, I started to see black and white before my eyes and felt that I was going to either pass out or wet my pants, or possibly both.

Suddenly I saw an open vision of the Lord beside me, and I heard Him say, *You know your clay, right?*

Still motionless, I responded, *Yes, Lord, but just get me out of here. I promise I'll be good.* And then He began walking toward the wheel. It was as though I clutched the hem of His garment and let Him pull me across that long stage. Finally I sat down at my potter's wheel and managed to say, "Hi!" to the audience. I did not know what else to do, so I began making a pot. I put the clay on the wheel, and as I added water and began to center the clay, I heard the living, audible voice of the Lord.

Oh, My child, I will never leave or forsake you.

My first response was, *What took You so long? What are You trying to do, kill me? I felt as though I would die of fright!* But I didn't want to get too mad because I didn't want Him to stop speaking. So I listened to His voice, and once again I portrayed God's heart while making a beautiful vessel.

As my hands went deep into the clay, He said, *I will pull up your walls* and *I will shape you* and *When you were in your mother's womb I knew you.* As I formed the clay into a pitcher, He said, *And you shall be my mouthpiece. I will glaze you blue with revelation and with the gold of My glory. I will send you to the nations to bring forth revival to My people.*

I shared His words for approximately fifteen minutes. Then I rose. As I walked back across the stage, I felt embarrassed that the audience stood and applauded loudly. It sure was not because I had stage presence. It was because the Holy Spirit came. The roar of the crowd filled the auditorium but I was so shy I could not even look up. Pastor Shackett wanted me to go back out and take a bow, but I shook my head and retreated backstage.

That is the story of how my journey into Master Potter Ministries began, birthed out of a broom closet many years ago. The Lord had told me that He would be opening doors for me, and that He wanted me simply to speak His heart. As I mentioned, I did not know this was prophecy. All I knew was that God would talk and I would listen and people would respond. He ambushed me that day in a muddy field, and my life was changed forever. I learned that God's dreams for me are much bigger than my dreams ever could be.

Yet I have not fully arrived. I am moving constantly toward my destiny. And so are you! God starts with us every day right where we are—using all of where we have been. The problem is, we lose sight of the movement in our calling. It is almost as if we begin living in pastel shades, not vibrant colors. We sometimes become satisfied with a muted version of what we are supposed to be. This is why we grow frustrated or disillusioned about fulfilling our destinies.

Do you realize that your life is not a mistake? God has ambushed you, too! It starts with God's dream for you. Everything starts with a dream. Creation started with a dream. And because we are created in the image of our Father, we are called to be creative dreamers.

Dreaming is wild and fun. In our heart of hearts, we would never choose a life that has no adventure. It is because of our fear and our smallness that we wind up seeking only what is "safe." We learn to value comfort and security. But what we call security is really insecurity and mediocrity. God wants us to take risks, to know the thrill and exhilaration of dreaming big.

Do you remember the parable of the talents? When the master returned, he commended the two servants who had taken a chance on increasing his holdings. "Well done!" he said. Another way he could have put it was, "Well risked!" God never punishes us when we dream big. When we are risking, we are coming alive. He looks on with delight when we walk over to someone in a restaurant or at work and pray for that person to be healed. Our risks thrill His heart. He wants us to dream big dreams. We can be in careers, retired, in school or stay-at-home moms or dads and still be entrepreneurs, holy revolutionaries and strategists. He is calling us to be "007" special-ops agents behind the scenes for Him. There are no limitations. With Jesus our potential is unrestricted.

Why is this so important for us to understand? Because the world is in crisis at every level. We are in an hour of great shaking and transition in our society. Daily we face terrorism, financial instability, attacks on the family, governmental upheavals, even destructive weather patterns. God has prepared us for this hour, which is full of great adventure and potential but also great danger. Each of us needs to pray and get fresh revelation with understanding for this critical time in history. We need to hear strategies from the counsels of God.

The enemy sees your potential. He knows that your life has God-ordained destiny. *Your dreams are dangerous to him.* If you embrace God's full purposes for your life, you will be a powerful weapon to defeat him and bring freedom to many.

What are the strategies the enemy uses to kill your dreams? That is the subject of the next chapter.

2

Dream Killers

Once we understand that we were born to be dreamers, we face the realization of how small and limited our dreams really are. We become so locked into mind-sets, strongholds, disappointments and hurts that we do not dream anymore. Why can't we dream? Why can't we play? Why can't we be creative? Actually, we can! We are creative by design. It is in our DNA; it is who we are. God created us to be creative.

Think about children at play. Before their instincts become squelched, before they are taught to think only in a linear fashion and creativity becomes minimized, their imaginations seem to splash with vibrant color all over the place. But as adults we think, *I'm not an artist; I'm not creative.* We fail to realize that creative imagination is not limited to the conventional forms of the arts. Unless we block it, creativity will flow from us—whether it is through problem solving, juggling family schedules, accounting or computer programming. We have believed the lie that we are not creative. And if we are not creative, then we have no heart for dreaming.

It is thrilling to watch the Holy Spirit bring new life to hearts that are open to His creative touch. Have you seen this? When I look at a room of people, I see visible signs as the Holy Spirit starts to fall. It is as though He comes as the master painter. Some people tremble and shake; others laugh or cry. Sometimes their faces glow with the light and glory of Jesus.

I remember one worship conference in the Midwest where the people welcomed the Holy Spirit among them. When I arrived they had already been worshiping for several hours. I was amazed to see that their faces were radiant and shining. Somehow the mystery of the glory of God was coming out of them. They were carriers of His splendor and beauty.

I was taken into an open vision, and I watched in awe as clouds of glory came out of their mouths, followed by swords. The Lord told me that as we worship Him, He will fight for us. In response, I saw the presence of darkness over the city begin to back away. Then I saw little fiery seeds of glory, like sparks crackling from a firecracker, enveloping the room. They were falling from the throne room on all these people. In the Spirit I also saw angels walking up and down the aisle, each one carrying a golden bowl. They were collecting the prayers and the worship of the saints and placing coals of fire on different individuals' mouths.

This is where life can get very exciting again. We will be talking later about becoming warriors for the Kingdom. These are soldiers who deal with a world that is shifting constantly. They expect the windows of heaven to open and God to meet them with revelation and mysteries. The presence and glory that they carry awakens conviction.

Do you know where their battle training starts? It starts with being childlike and willing to dream again. In fact it is almost impossible to awaken a heart that cannot dream. We must get past the lies that want to surface every time we try to move forward. We must deal once and for all with the negativity that has plagued us our entire lives. We need to say, "The dream killers are not going to stop me. I am not listening to those who say that it is impossible or that it will cost too much money or that I don't have the talent to accomplish it. I am going to give it a try anyway." We start moving, and we find that we have creative instinct after all.

Facing the Dream Killers

A number of dream killers are described in this chapter. Perhaps some of them will sound uncomfortably familiar. Be willing to open your heart and understand how they have been operating. It is time to be a David, load your slingshot and kill the Goliaths in your life.

We Hide behind Excuses

An obvious dream killer is one that we might call a "natural" hindrance, a problem that we face in life: "I can't speak. . . . I'm not smart enough. . . . I'm shy and lack people skills. . . . I'm a single parent. . . . I'm not a leader. . . . I'm not talented enough. . . . I'm too old. . . . " Insert your own natural disability—your excuse—that you think keeps you from your dreams.

Our tendency is to look at these hindrances and say, "I would like to do such and such, but I have this problem," or, "The world values thus and so, and I'm not like that, so I guess I'm out." We look at these excuses and limitations and disqualify ourselves.

God never does that. He says, "I know the thoughts and plans that I have for you . . . thoughts and plans for welfare and peace and not for evil, to give you hope in your final outcome" (Jeremiah 29:11, AMPLIFIED). He puts the dreams in our hearts, and then He wants to take us on the journey to walk those dreams out. Remember, our dreamer God has bigger dreams for our lives than we do. Sometimes He has to ambush us to get us to our destinations as we travel through the seasons of our lives.

When I was a child I was tongue-tied and dyslexic, so I could not pronounce certain words. I always admired healing evangelist Kathryn Kuhlman because she also had dyslexia. That is why she talked so slowly, so she could get the words out correctly. Yet she stood before the masses and moved in signs, wonders and miracles. It is the irony of God that He takes unlikely people and does supernatural things with them.

We Are Afraid to Have Fun

Let's face it: "Religion" isn't fun. Legalism shuts down the human heart and closes off intimacy with God. All too often our churches maintain a form of religion without the power of His presence.

The "religious system" sometimes gives the message that rest and relaxation are unspiritual and unnecessary. Jesus did not come to earth, however, to set up a religious system. He came to establish deep relationships. I believe that He wants us to understand that walking with Him is a journey of excitement, which involves having fun!

If you have a child or a grandchild, a nephew or a niece, who loves to spend time with you—taking walks, going on boat rides, gardening—you tend to get more engaged. When you have fun together, your relationship grows. It is like that with God. He is eager to interact with us. He is longing to be fully engaged with us in everyday life.

We are the ones who stop the game. "Time-out!" we yell, just when it is getting good. We prefer not to play because it does not look spiritual. We also tend to think that if we are too lighthearted, we have done something wrong. We are harder on ourselves than God is. He wants us to have fun and play again.

Every journey has ups and downs. There will be times of difficulty and suffering as well as times of joy and celebration. We expect seasons of pain in the Christian walk, but we need to expect times of pleasure and passion, as well. It is not an either/or situation. We embrace the journey and celebrate life.

We Live in a Fantasy World

What if our lives turn out to be totally different from our dreams?

Some people are so disappointed with the "now" that they live in a fantasy world. Others live vicariously through somebody else's life or dreams. Still others say, "If this is my destiny, then God made a really big mistake." It is too depressing for them to look at their own lives so they give up. They reason like this: "My dreams don't mean anything. I didn't get ____. I believed God for ____, and that hasn't happened, either. Look at those people and all they have."

Do you feel that way? It shows a crisis of trust in God! It means that you probably do not understand what you have been given, who you really are and how God sees you. If we grasped how much God genuinely loves us, if we could see ourselves through His eyes, our lives would be dramatically different. We would know who we are and what our purpose is. I can assure you that we would live very differently, love extravagantly and pray strategically.

Your journey is not a storybook picture; it is not a fantasy. It is what is in your world right now. Once upon a time is *now*. Happily ever after is *now*. What is around you? Who are the people with you? Your prince is there—He is the

Lord! All the storybook characters are there—and they look a lot like your sometimes-healthy, sometimes-dysfunctional friends and relatives.

If things do not look the way you imagined they would be, then in your mind you have built a fantasy: "This is my ideal job; this is my ideal mate; these are my ideal children." Your ideal children are the ones that you already have. Your ideal job is the one you have—*now.* You are in process: What are you doing with the material God has given you to work with?

We Accept False Labels

Counterfeit labels give the appearance of the real thing, but they are cheap imitations. In the case of dream killers, this means losing sight of the fact that you are an original, custom designed by God, and accepting the false assessment that you were made in a sweatshop.

Labels have to do with unwritten rules. It happens like this. You have a calling from God, but you never seem to be put into a place to let it grow. Perhaps you are divorced and your church frowns on divorce. Or you are married, but your spouse is not saved. Or you are single, and your church is not comfortable putting single people in positions of leadership—particularly a single woman. Or perhaps you feel on the outskirts because you are in a racial minority or are elderly or your son is homosexual.

Whatever the reason for the labels that are put on us, we see others positioned ahead of us—the young couples, the financially well-off, the popular—and our hearts faint. We compare ourselves with others, and jealousy shuts us down. We think, *I'll never be able to fulfill my dream. I'm disqualified by the system.*

The Lord goes beyond labels when He gives out marching orders. We could name many people in Scripture who defied convention, some of them pairing with other candidates who were just as unlikely. Simeon was an old priest and Anna was an old widow and prophetess, but the two of them were brought together in an assignment to announce the arrival of the Messiah. Esther, an orphaned Jewish girl, teamed up with Mordecai, her cousin, and delivered the Jewish nation from destruction. Deborah was a judge and prophetess during a time when Israel was being harshly oppressed. She teamed with Barak, a great military commander, and, with the courageous efforts of a housewife named Jael, their enemy was destroyed.

All of these characters ignored conventional labels that could have disqualified them to achieve great things: age, marital status, race, sex, job descriptions. Because they were not afraid to dream, God could give them creative and dangerous assignments.

We Fear Becoming Proud

I read recently that the king of Norway apologized to the world for winning so many gold medals at one of the Winter Olympics. I have a Scandinavian background and recognized the inner message: He did not want the other nations to think that Norwegians consider themselves better than anyone else.

Something similar happens in church: False humility keeps everyone small and "average." It is quite demeaning. It is part of the religious spirit that minimizes people and destroys their dreams. If people have vision for their lives and stick their heads up to pursue something significant, then they are criticized for being proud. In fact, those who do stand out will be taught a lesson in humility by having their heads cut off so they remain even with everybody else. Those who are afraid of others' gifting are usually insecure, competitive and jealous and want ownership of the anointing of God.

We need to have heroes of the faith—sports figures, artists, entertainers, politicians, educators, inventors—extraordinary Christians who are trendsetters and history shakers. We need gifted people who can have an impact on the global scene. Why *not* have big dreams? People's gifts open doors for them so they can stand before "kings" and give testimony to their faith.

This dream killer squelches any hope of vibrant living. It is like killing ourselves—a slow poisoning—because we are not being who we were created to be. Who benefits from this? Not us and not other people, only the enemy of our souls. We become miserable and we make other people miserable.

We Get Angry at God

"My life is so bad." "Where was God when I needed Him?" "He must be a cruel God if this is what I'm saddled with—a loveless marriage." "My child is so sick. I can't bear to live like this."

Sometimes when real life comes, we get angry because we do not understand what is happening or why. Scripture tells us that "hope deferred makes the heart sick" (Proverbs 13:12). We look at our pain and cannot imagine surviving even one more day. Loved ones did not get healed. Rebellious children break our hearts. The hope for marriage from a prophetic word given twenty years ago has not happened.

The enemy deceives us into thinking that God is responsible for our conditions, so we find ourselves backing away from Him and filling our lives with substitutions. Ours is a medicated society; we do not want to feel anything that is painful. So just like those who abuse alcohol or drugs, we medicate our hearts by shutting down and not feeling. It takes care of the pain, at least temporarily. This gives the enemy an enormous advantage. He hates us and wants to kill us, but he is too cunning to be so obvious.

This is a call to action. When we walk in the valleys, we have a decision to make. Our pain can make us wither, or it can awaken our hearts to be passionately real. Our losses can destroy us, or they can help us grow stronger. Our actions can feed the devil's victimization of our lives, or they can point to the Word of God.

True dreamers will take their anger to the foot of the cross where they will find a heart big enough to hold their pain. They will begin to understand who God is and what He thinks about them.

We Find Delays Painful

Let's reframe time. Most people want to forget the past, but every moment of our lives has a purpose in God's plan. Not only does the past hold losses and regrets, it also marks celebrations of the present and hope for the future. It is the weaving of the tapestry of who we are.

This means that there is an odd truth about our destinies. Have you spotted it? It is this: The journey is actually our destiny. We sometimes fall into the trap of waiting to arrive somewhere instead of living right where we are. If our place of arriving is always down the road, we will never get there.

In other words, our destiny is not far away in the future, a somewhere-over-the-rainbow thing. We are living in the present, a time frame that integrates with the past, even as we are birthing the future. This is happening all at the same time, in a single moment. It is as though the different time layers collide: We see glimpses of the future even as we live in the present and pull stones of remembrance into view.

Time marks the realm of man; eternity marks the realm of God. This means that we can have many dreams happening in different stages, all at the same time. Multiple pregnancies and multiple births are not a problem for God. We are always in places of transition, ever changing and growing.

But what do we do? We decide that we do not want to wait.

Waiting kills our flesh, and it purifies our motives. Waiting is never a waste of time because God is always working out what we are waiting for. His timetable is not like ours. Forty years is not a long time in God's mind. For us, with our microwave mentality, forty minutes is a very long time. We want it in thirty seconds! We call it delay; God calls it perfect timing. We call it slow; God calls it just right. Training for reigning is a prophetic journey, a dramatic saga that lasts a lifetime. There is always something percolating in the spiritual realm. We do not always see it in the natural, and if we get impatient and try to finish the job ourselves, our dreams may suffer.

God wants to partner with us in our dreams. He gives us the ability to think, to imagine, to create, and then He visits us with the gentle whispering of His still small voice—all the while teaching us to trust His perfect timing.

We Become Spectators in the Grandstands

I have been watching an interesting and unhealthy shift in the Body of Christ. Perhaps you have noticed this, too—especially if you are over forty. Those of us in the older generation are being encouraged to grab our pom-poms and cheer on the younger generation. This looks good at the outset; we must support our young people. But there is a problem slipping in unnoticed.

The current emphasis on the younger generation is causing many people to encourage them—at the price of our own dreams and destiny. The result is that we are not training and mentoring our young people; we are stepping aside to let them take our places. We have abdicated our positions with both God and man. This is not always easy to spot because it is wrapped in good intentions, but we are being disobedient to God's calls on our own lives.

The Church today should not be seeking a "youth movement." Rather, we should be cheering for a generational anointing. God's heart calls for blended dreams in the generations. Look at Abraham, Isaac and Jacob: God sees the whole family! All of the generations need to come together for a common cause.

Do you know how an enemy destroys a vast army? By shooting the generals and other high-ranking officers. And the best way to shoot them in the Church is to abort their dreams and take away their authority and their voice. The "older" Christians have reached the place where they have credibility and influence. At this point they should have maturity, character and stability. Because they have survived many wars, they also have insight into battles that the young people are facing today.

The youth are looking for models and mentors. They are eager to learn from those who have experience in doing exploits and taking territory. They are like young soldiers in training. But the generals have filed up into the grandstands and joined the other spectators.

What is keeping the officers glued to their seats? Many think that God has passed over them, because most of the prophetic words are for the youth. A lot of them are looking at their losses, regrets and dashed dreams. They fear that their best years are over, and they get depressed. They feel invalidated. They have become disillusioned and disappointed. Adding to the pain is the realization that they are weak physically or feel as though their bodies are falling apart. The challenges of modern technology are intimidating, too.

The biggest lie they hear from the enemy is that they are beyond the point of having something to give. They no longer believe that they have a baton to pass on; it is more like a dried-up stick. They rationalize, "I've done my part. Here comes a generation that is so alive and energetic. I'll just cheer it on. At least I'm doing *something*." In other words, their dreams are dying. No longer do they hold the sword of the Lord that is dripping with the blood of the enemies of the cross. Instead, the old generals are all sitting back drinking coffee while the youth go out to war.

We can learn an important lesson from King David's catastrophic "retiring" from battle. During one spring, the time when kings went out to battle, he stayed home and sent others out to war. What happened? He fell into sexual sin with another man's wife. In a time of promotion and great transition, the enemy loves to disqualify leaders who could have great impact on their world.

Are you one of these officers? This should be your finest hour. Remember that no one needs to give up any dreams in order to help somebody else. If you are in a season of transition, then come forth with new strength for the Lamb's war.

We Are Afraid to Be Real

A dream killer that is rarely talked about involves secrets—family secrets. There is a code of honor in most families that is generally unspoken but understood: You do not reveal certain family issues. What would people think if they knew? These secrets must stay buried forever. The family members must wear masks to hide their true feelings and pretend that everything is all right. On the outside friends and neighbors see the perfect family, the perfect career, the illusion of the perfect life.

The truth is, everything is not all right. Fear isolates the family members from each other and everyone else. Unable to share the truth, many people feel that they are the only ones who are dealing with such raw issues: adultery, domestic abuse, abortion, Internet pornography, all kinds of uncontrollable addictions—the list goes on. No one must *ever* find out. The shame and betrayal would be more unbearable than the pain of denial.

Living in silence is a living death. No dream can survive it. When life itself is a prison, only the intense and unconditional love of God can bring us out. He can heal the deepest places of a lonely soul. "I will never leave or forsake you," He says, and hope begins to seem possible.

We are all on a journey of healing. It is a progression as the Lord awakens our hearts to dream again. We need to remember that the truth will set us free—and Jesus is the truth. He will expose the darkness and help us live in reality, not hiddenness. As we learn to be more genuine, others will respond.

I saw this principle unfold dramatically in my own family. Actually it is possible that most of these dream killers were at work in my family! I want to share a story with you briefly to illustrate the importance of being set free from the most common dream killer of all: unforgiveness.

We Struggle with Forgiveness

Unforgiveness is one of the most influential dream killers in our lives. Its crippling effect can lock us into areas that we are not even aware of. Some of the biggest wounds, those that require the deepest level of forgiveness, come from those who are closest to us.

My parents got divorced when I was twelve years old. Since I was a child of the sixties, we never talked about it. One of my family secrets was that my dad, who was going to medical school at the time, was an alcoholic. Another secret was the adulterous affair he was having with another medical student.

Of his four children, my father seemed to have particular animosity toward me. My mother told me many years later that he hated me because I looked so much like him. And he, too, had dyslexia. I suppose he transferred his self-hatred to me. I only knew at the time that he was physically and verbally abusive, a hard taskmaster whom I could not please. We all had to get good grades and never get dirty while playing or his temper would flare. We had to look the part of the perfect family.

My father became a successful doctor, but he abandoned our family both financially and emotionally. As an adult I forgave him many times with a "blanket prayer" of forgiveness, but I did not realize that the wound went much deeper.

I was in my thirties and in full-time ministry when the Lord ambushed me. He spoke to me about this issue of forgiveness and told me to call my dad, which was the last thing I wanted to do. I had not seen him once in twenty years.

But God set up a divine appointment for both of us. While God was healing areas of my heart, He was simultaneously bringing salvation to my dad. God's timing was perfect.

I was amazed at the extent to which God went to give me the opportunity for deeper forgiveness. It began with the continual prompting to try to reach my dad by phone. I wrestled with this for days. I finally decided to send up a fleece. I would try information. If they had his number, I would call him. They had his number.

That conversation yielded the news that my dad was in the hospital and dying of bone cancer. I was unaware that he was even sick. The doctor I spoke with at the hospital said that he had only a few months to live.

I was on the road at this time and wondered if I should cancel my ministry commitments for that week and go see him. The doctor assured me that he would be just fine. But the Lord had other ideas. That night He gave me a prophetic dream.

In the dream I was walking through a town with cobble-stone streets. Two huge angels were walking on either side of me. They took me to the very edge of the town to a train station. I looked inside and there on a wooden bench sat my dad. I knew that the death train was coming and that he was going to die. I wanted to go to him but the angels barred the way. When I awoke sobbing, I knew that it was now or never. The next day I cancelled my ministry trip and got on a plane.

I arrived at the cancer ward and went to the nurses' station. They were glad to see me. His second wife had allowed no visitors for six weeks. He had been dying all alone. When I walked into his room and first saw him, I did not know if he would even recognize me. I was surprised at how old and thin he looked; he was all yellow and riddled with cancer. He was no longer the big, angry man I remembered from my childhood.

"Hi, Daddy. Daddy, this is Jill. Do you remember me? I am your number two daughter."

He sat up in bed and started to cry. He said, "Jill, Jill, I'm dying."

"Yes, I know." Then I said, "Daddy, you know we got ripped off. I haven't seen you in all these years. We can't have those lost years, but we can have eternity together. I have a friend whom I want you to meet. Do you want to meet my Jesus?"

As tears were falling down his cheeks, he said, "Yes, I would like that."

He could barely talk but he repeated these words after me: "Jesus, forgive me. I'm a sinner. I want You as my Lord and my Savior." So my dad was born into the Kingdom of God.

I looked at him and knew there was more I had to say. "Daddy, you know what? I have hated you. You deserted me. You left me. I needed you. Daddy, would you forgive me for being so angry and so bitter?"

He began to cry and said, "Sweetheart, I forgive you. Will you forgive *me*? I didn't know how to be a dad to you. I am so sorry that you got hurt."

As we embraced, the wall of separation came down. It was the first time I felt loved by him and connected to him.

The next day I brought a decorated Christmas tree to his room. He was sitting up in bed and now his countenance had changed: There was a glow of the Lord about him. He could barely talk, but every once in a while he would say, "Oh, Jill, you are so beautiful."

I would respond, "Oh, Daddy, tell me again!"

On the third day the Lord woke me up at four in the morning to go to the hospital. When I opened the door to his room I could sense a spirit of death. I was horrified to see him gasping for air with blood coming out of his mouth. I ran over to him and as I laid hands on him, I could feel the power of God shoot into him. I said, "Daddy, it's time to go home. It's time to go home to Jesus." I embraced him and said, "I love you. I have come to tell you good-bye." He died in my arms.

The first person to hear this story was my mother. She was shocked to see me and then hear that my dad had accepted the Lord. She started weeping, because she still loved him, and said, "Now I know that Jesus is real!" It was so clearly of God's doing that it witnessed to her of His power and love in a way that nothing else could have.

All of us have been hurt, rejected and disappointed. Every single one of us has a history. We can all look back and think of one or two individuals who have broken our hearts. But Jesus says that we have to forgive. It is a choice. It is out of obedience and loving Jesus that we forgive.

When we forgive, the deep roots of anger, bitterness and resentment are pulled out. Every seed that is not planted by the Father needs to be uprooted. We put it all at the cross of Jesus Christ. We need to be able to say, "Jesus, because this person hurt me, I got angry. I got resentful. I put walls up. Please forgive me for how I have hurt that person and how I protected myself."

Then we need to have mercy and say, "Jesus, not only do I forgive that person, but I extend blessing. I release that person. Lord, I choose to be healthy and no longer feel like a victim. I want to be an overcomer—and a dreamer once more."

It Is Time for a Jailbreak!

Why do people quit dreaming? They are trying to live without the pain of dashed hopes, but that is a bigger sorrow than not dreaming. Not living and not taking risks that help them reach their destinies is a living death. Is anyone disqualified from dreaming? No. Should anyone quit because it seems too hard? No.

I feel that a huge release is coming in the days ahead in the area of dreams and destinies. God is calling radical men and women to do astounding exploits. They will be deliverers and revolutionaries. Part of their journey is to have the courage to take the divine assignments and live their dreams to the fullest.

This is a message that needs to be shouted from the housetops! We must not only follow our dreams but also come alongside others and encourage them. We need to speak destiny to them. A lot of people have no idea what their destinies are. They just mark time. Scripture tells us that without a vision the people perish. But as soon as they hear a prophetic word that reveals their callings and their destinies, watch them. They will look like a closed flower blossoming in the sunlight. They will have vision and energy and passion to do something because they have received more insight and revelation about who they are.

The gradual unfolding of their journeys awakens them to live again.

It is a thrilling and challenging place. I never thought I would minister in the way God has called me, but He kept urging me: *Do you love Me? Are you willing to risk? Are you willing to die to yourself? Will you give a word of encouragement to someone?*

It is like a jailbreak and you must be part of it. Let God reveal any area in your life where you have been imprisoned by a dream killer. It might start with your perception of yourself: your self-talk, your self-love, your self-hatred. Ask His forgiveness. Ask Him to create a clean heart in you and fill it with His love. When you understand what God thinks of you, even in your brokenness, you begin to embrace the idea of loving yourself. That is the time for the jailbreak because you know you have value and so do your dreams.

God loves it when we dream. It is as though He has given us paints and put a canvas before us. "There," He says with a smile. "Paint!" As we will discover in the next chapter, He can hardly wait to see what we will come up with.

3

Your Wildest Imagination

In Psalm 37:4 we find beautiful words of promise for those learning to dream:

> Delight yourself also in the Lord, and He shall give you the desires of your heart.

We read here the longing to empty ourselves and receive from God's hand whatever He chooses to give us. And that interpretation is a fitting place to start. When you delight in someone, as we delight in and love the Lord, you make yourself vulnerable to that person. You want what that person wants.

The problem, however, is that we miss the deeper meaning of verses like this one. We stop short of the interactive nature of love. We think that we are to empty ourselves of all personal desires or the uniqueness of how God created us and do only what He wants us to do. But that is not interesting to God. He has given us creativity, and He finds great pleasure in watching us grow in our gifting. In other words, because He loves us, the almighty, eternal, omniscient, omnipotent God is willing to entertain *our* desires. God says, "What do you want? Tell Me your dreams. Let's dance the dance of your destiny together."

Scott, a friend of mine, relayed a delightful conversation he had with God about the journey to one of his dreams:

> I was living in Los Angeles at the time, and I hated it. I wanted to move to the mountains. So I decided to ask God about it.
>
> I said, "Is it okay, God?"
>
> He said, *What do you want?*
>
> So I responded with what I thought would please Him: "What do *You* want?"
>
> He said, *No, what do* you *want?*
>
> I was getting perplexed. "No, Lord," I said, "what do You want for me?"
>
> And God said, *No, what do* you *want?*
>
> I was not getting anywhere so I decided to answer His question. "Okay, God," I said. "You know I hate L.A. I love the people, but I don't want to live here. I would love to live up in the beautiful mountains and go fly-fishing."
>
> He said, *I will go with you.*
>
> When He said that, I was on the Pomona freeway, driving through Los Angeles. The thick presence of God filled the car as I wept all the way through Los Angeles. That conversation changed my life.

We get caught in the trap that says, "I just want what God wants." We forget that He has created us with minds so we can think and imagine and dream. He wants to partner with us in that creative process. This partnering is shown among the earliest stories in the Bible. When God gave Adam the job of naming the animals, He did not say, "Adam, here is a lion and here is a bear." He said, "Okay, Adam. Here are the animals I have made. What are you going to name them?" I believe that God watched with delight as Adam, discovering his own creative soul, partnered with the Creator.

We are not robots! We are passionate people living a custom-designed destiny. And we are moving along with a creative God who has extraordinary plans for our lives. He keeps the adventure going by unfolding the living tapestry of our lives moment by moment. It goes back to identity. You and I are created in the likeness and image of God, who has a great imagination. As royal children of the dreamer Father, we belong to a different Kingdom, one that is wild and free. There is something about living in the Spirit that is the truest kind of living.

So it is okay to have a vision of what we would like our ministry or our business to look like. Actually, I think that those dreams really started with Him; He is the source of everything good: "Every good gift and every perfect gift is from above, and comes down from the Father of lights, with whom there is no variation or shadow of turning" (James 1:17). If He puts a creative spark within us and also gives us the ability to dream with complete freedom, then He will come alongside us and help us, because that is part of His desire, as well.

God *loves* us. He always dreams bigger dreams for us than we dream for ourselves. This is why some dreams never seem to come true—not because we should not dream them, but because they are only a small part of the bigger dreams that fulfill our longings completely.

I believe that this is one of the keys to understanding and enduring suffering. What do you do when so much of the Bible talks about suffering? You trust Him in the valleys and keep your eyes on the mountaintops. God never abandons us; He positions us in the directions of our destinies.

I love the story of Joseph. It shows this journey of dreaming through times of promotion and times of suffering so clearly. It is a gripping saga that touches the human soul on almost every emotional level—treachery and betrayal, forgiveness and reconciliation, hate and love. It is a roller-coaster journey of how God prepares someone for great authority and privilege.

Let's take a look at the parallels for our own lives.

Joseph: From Dungeon to Destiny

Joseph was a young man destined to be a deliverer. We know the story of how he was favored by his father among his eleven brothers and given a beautiful multicolored coat. That coat was a reflection of the multifaceted gifting in his life. It also represented the mantle of blessing and authority his father was passing down to him.

> Now Israel [Jacob's name had been changed to *Israel*] loved Joseph more than all his children, because he was the son of his old age. Also he made him a tunic of many colors. But when his brothers saw that their father loved him more than all his brothers, they hated him and could not speak peaceably to him.
>
> Now Joseph had a dream [in which his brothers bowed down before him], and he told it to his brothers; and they hated him even more.
>
> Genesis 37:3–5

Joseph was a dreamer. He was also a prophet. At seventeen he dreamed his destiny, literally, but he did not have revelation of how this would come to pass. Unfortunately, when leaders show someone favoritism and that person moves in the gifts of the Spirit, it usually stirs jealousy and competition among the "brothers."

And there is always the question of timing. Joseph blurted out his dreams of supremacy not once but twice, including having authority over his parents the second time. Even Jacob looked askance at that!

Have you ever shared a prophetic promise in the wrong timing? You learn after a while not to do that. Why? Because it stirs up jealousy. And if it is left unchecked, jealousy always befriends murder in some degree. People rarely say, "Oh! We have been waiting for you all our lives! We are so excited that you have received revelation from God on how to run the church. Yes, we know you are only seventeen, but, please, come into the office."

Does God use young people? Of course. But the hangman's noose of the prophetic is timing. Often what you see is correct but you do not yet have revelation to know how it is to be applied. That is part of the school of the Holy Spirit. Sometimes the Lord tells you to speak out. Other times you are supposed to ponder things in your heart, maybe for years.

When you reveal a promise before God's timetable calls for it, even good people who love the Father can come against you. So the brothers tore off Joseph's colorful robe of authority, threw him into a pit and sold him into slavery.

Another Garment Change

This might not look like the road to destiny, but God is always in charge of the bigger picture. Scripture says that the boy was bought by Potiphar, the captain of Pharaoh's guard, and eventually made overseer of Potiphar's entire household. The Lord blessed Joseph and "made all he did to prosper" (Genesis 39:3).

In the midst of this pagan culture with his dream nowhere in sight, Joseph still followed God. As the years passed, he held to his testimony. It seemed that things were beginning to fall into place; he was living on the mountaintop. Then one day Joseph was betrayed by Potiphar's wife—and, again, the Lord allowed it. You see, Potiphar's house was not the right place strategically for Joseph. His robe of authority was ripped off once again, and the false accusation of being a rapist sent him to prison. But this was not just any prison. It was the royal dungeon that God would use for divine appointments with the baker and cupbearer. It was a transition that would lead to his being positioned in the palace.

' Have there been times in your life when the Lord has shifted and changed your circumstances? Perhaps you were uprooted out of your home, your job or your city. Perhaps you are a pastor, a worship leader or an intercessor. You had favor among the people and thought you would be in that church forever. Then competition and control, hallmarks of jealousy, drove you out.

· This is part of the prophetic journey for someone moving in his or her destiny. A king can be put into place in a day, but the one who lets his imagination spark his dreams will go through the fires of God to be trained. The reason for this is clear: When you let your heart awaken to your dreams, you will wear not only the beautiful colored robe of God's favor and blessing, but also a garment of humility and meekness with the glory going to the Lord.

Prison to Palace

Thirteen years had passed since Joseph's brothers had sold him into slavery. He was now thirty years old (see Genesis 41:46). He had matured; he had grown wise; and he had gained a reputation for interpreting dreams. God's favor was with him, and another transition was about to happen. Unexpectedly Joseph found himself rocketing from the valley of despair to the mountaintop of fulfilled dreams. In one day he went from prison to a position of authority second only to Pharaoh himself—from dungeon to destiny!

Not only did Joseph interpret Pharaoh's dreams, but now he knew what to do with that knowledge. He gave application to the strategies that the Lord had given him. God shifted Joseph into a place of wealth and influence so that now, wearing fine garments and gold jewelry, Joseph could set laws in motion to grow and store immeasurable amounts of grain. This food would save not only Israel but all the nations on earth stricken by the famine.

Do you see the pattern? Can you relate this to experiences in your own life? There are many types of "foreign lands" with many mountains and valleys. Perhaps you dreamed of a happy marriage but your husband is not following the Lord. Or maybe the ministry your heart desires is always out of reach. Have you been betrayed and misunderstood? The Lord has allowed even that to test your heart. Are you still seeking Him or are you starting to compromise a little? Are you not quite as "on fire" for God as you used to be? Is your dream fading or does your imagination still soar? Are you bitter or sweet?

So far this journey of Joseph still does not look like the dream he was holding on to, but God was with him, step by step. Psalm 105 says that God allowed the famine that brought Joseph's family to Egypt years later. In time Joseph's family did indeed bow down before him, justifying his dream. But because he partnered with God, his destiny was even greater than he had imagined.

> Moreover He called for a famine in the land; He destroyed all the provision of bread. He sent a man before them—Joseph—who was sold as a slave. They hurt his feet with fetters, he was laid in irons. Until the time that his word came to pass, the word of the LORD tested him. The king sent and released him, the ruler of the people let him go free. He made him lord of his house, and ruler of all his possessions, to bind his princes at his pleasure, and teach his elders wisdom.
>
> Psalm 105:16–22

In others words, it was *God* who set the world up for international crisis. He is doing it again today—crisis such as we have never seen before. He is the One who will stop the rains, bring the earthquakes, shake the governments. He is also the One who will put godly men and women strategically into place as they hold on to their dreams.

Do you feel as though you have been in a dungeon for so long you think He has forgotten about you? As with Joseph, God is preparing you in secret and could in a moment put you on a world platform. Do not let your heart faint when your finest hour is about to emerge.

God is looking for new "Josephs"—those who are not only prophetic but also strategic thinkers, those who know how to mobilize people and plan finances on a global scale. Joseph oversaw the transfer of wealth during a worldwide famine. Through his leadership, Egypt became a superpower in the world economy—and delivered millions from starvation.

Jesus said that as the last days unfold, we will witness an increase in war, turmoil and natural disasters (see Matthew 24:6–8; Luke 21:10–11). As the judgments come to pass, God will raise up cities of refuge. These cities will be sanctuaries, places of healing where worship, culture, education and industry thrive—even in the midst of dark and perilous times.

Pharaoh gave Joseph and the Israelites the best land in Egypt, the land of Goshen, their city of refuge (see Genesis 47:6). And while those around them were selling livestock and lands and ultimately their own freedom to buy bread, the people of Israel were growing in number and prospering.

The Israelites entered Egypt as a family; in Goshen they became a nation.

The Power of Forgiveness

Notice that Joseph was not given dreams as a boy about being sold into slavery and ending up in irons in the dungeon. God did not tell him everything at the beginning of his journey. Joseph received only the revelation that someday his family was going to bow down to him. He made mistakes and he suffered cruelties, but he never let his dream die. That is why God could fulfill his destiny.

When his brothers fell prostrate before him, Joseph had already forgiven them in his heart. He understood that God had sent him as a forerunner to save his family. When he finally revealed his identity to them, he said, "Do not therefore be grieved or angry with yourselves because you sold me here; for God sent me before you to preserve life" (Genesis 45:5).

You see, there are two seats in heaven. There is the judgment seat and the mercy seat. When you are bleeding from betrayal and false accusations, you will discover that the accuser is also condemning you before the judgment seat. He is pouring out partial truths and some distortions. You have to watch that unforgiveness and bitterness do not grow. Otherwise your wounds will become "infected" and you could be disqualified from moving forward.

Rather, go to the mercy seat. Throw yourself between the horns of the altar and on the precious splattered blood of Jesus, saying, "Lord, forgive me. Forgive those who have risen up against me." Your wounds will begin to heal and the scars will begin to glow with the resurrection anointing of Jesus. Then when you go to the city gates you can speak with authority because you have forgiven. You can declare, "Open up the gates so that the King of glory can come in!"

You might be stuck in a job as a salesclerk, divorced with a couple of kids, driving a worn-out little car, but your heart aches to open a flower shop. Or you might be a high-powered executive with heavy responsibilities, but you have longed for years to be on the mission field. You have to face certain realities, but what is your dream? And whom are you touching even today? What is God urging you to be creative about? Taking a night class? Supporting a short-term mission trip? Writing poetry? Maybe you love to preach. Well, what if your platform is different from the usual platform? How multidimensional is your world? Do you see your world with different doorways and portals and opportunities? Or is it a prison?

No matter what your limitations in the natural realm, just take the next step. Let your imagination soar from where you are. Whatever circumstances you have to work with, begin. All you have to do is take one step toward it. That is where God meets you. If you stand back and say, "I'm waiting on God to do such and such so I can do this," then you never will. Destiny has everything to do with movement.

Let's cry out for heaven to invade earth, for God's radical Kingdom to invade our clay vessels. Let's say, "Awaken me, Lord, to partnering with You. Even though I don't see the big picture, I have hope. I want to dream."

There is one dream we all share, though we may not always be aware of it. It is a dream that speaks of the longing of the Church: an intimate relationship with Jesus, our Bridegroom King. Let's turn our hearts now to discover what it means to love.

Part Two

LOVERS

As the bridegroom rejoices over the bride, so shall your God rejoice over you.

Isaiah 62:5

4

In Search of a Bride

The Church is in transition. The dreamers in her midst are willing to lose everything to gain everything. They are willing to embrace the challenge, to climb the mountain. It is risky, but they are saying, "I'm moving forward no matter what." And you have joined them! You know you are going to get beaten up on the way, but it does not matter. You are choosing to follow your destiny.

Here we have this untamable, passionate, wild dreamer of a God, and His Church is growing with the desire for fresh "God encounters." What we had before, whatever signs and wonders, whatever our experiences, was good, but now we want more. It is all about passion and risk, which is faith. In other words, we are hungry for God.

During a time of teaching and ministry that I led recently, I noticed a young woman named Gretchen who had been weeping for hours. At one point in the gathering I spoke with her and was astonished by what she had experienced. This is what she told me:

> I had a vision of Jesus, but I couldn't see His face. I was crying out to be able to see His face. After the meeting was over, I tried to leave but I couldn't. I started crying and went deeper into the Lord and His presence. My arms started hurting. They felt as though they were on fire. I started to try and put it out; it felt as if my flesh was burning. Then my knees started burning. In a vision, I could see myself catching on fire. I was trying to put the fire out because it hurt. Then, I just became engulfed in flames. My hair caught on fire; all of me caught on fire. I was terrified. I could see this vision of myself burning with my eyes open or shut.
> It was terrifying; but I really liked it, too!
> I think it meant that the Lord was consuming me and that He was burning away my flesh. That's why it was so terrifying and why it hurt so badly. After I was aflame, He kind of threw me into this bigger flame. This word burst out of me: "This is the fire; this is the fire of God. This is what happens when you seek My face." I believe that means that whenever you seek the face of Jesus, when you seek Him with your whole heart, He will consume you and burn away your flesh and bring you closer to Him.

A lot of times when I have had visitations with the Lord, I have seen things that deal with fire. There are different kinds of fires, but many times it comes like a refiner's fire as He burns off the dross. As the fire gets hotter and more intense, it becomes "cleaner" and brilliant white—the glory fire—and we start to move into the deeper things of God. We become consumed with longing for Him.

But let's back up for a moment. How did we get to this place of longing for deeper intimacy?

Setting Hearts on Fire

Before any dream was ever dreamed or any longing for Jesus ever realized, the Holy Spirit was at work. Why? Because the Father had commissioned Him. What was and is on the Father's heart? To get a Bride for His Son. The Holy Spirit, then, is the One who awakens and sets the dreamers' hearts on fire for our glorious Bridegroom King. It is through the Holy Spirit that the Bride is prepared, nurtured and trained. It is also through the Holy Spirit that we start to feel the love of the Son.

How does the Holy Spirit do this? He brings illumination, revelation, comfort. He is a teacher, an equipper. He is also our friend. If we settle into the idea that because we have the gift of tongues we have the Holy Spirit, we will not move into the intimate relationship that the Father desires us to have with Jesus. Nor will we ever open up the heavens, because the Holy Spirit is the one who directs us how to move in anointing.

We are in a season of war, and in the spiritual realm one thing about war is clear: If we are going to survive this wilderness and reach our destinies, we need to be in relationship with the Holy Spirit. He is the One who brings revelation of the Father and Son. Our cry should be: "Awaken us, Lord. We want to partner with You. We want to have deeper understanding of who You are."

When the Holy Spirit comes into a meeting, He comes with purposes and plans; He has an assignment from the Father. It is not a trivial thing that the Holy Spirit shows up. When He arrives He breaks in with the purposes of heaven for our destinies. He awakens our hearts to Jesus' love for us.

These are radical encounters! Yet, do you know what sometimes happens? The Holy Spirit comes and we do not even talk to Him. We ignore Him because we are too busy with our agendas. Do we say, "Holy Spirit, what do You

71

have?" Or do we say, "Excuse me, but we have ten worship songs on our list and this is not the time for healing.
Do You mind following the program?" We grieve Him and
shut Him down. We want Him only when it is convenient
and makes us look anointed.

Even when we do move beyond our own agendas and
say we want the gifts He brings, do we want those *things* or
do we want *Him*? Granted, we are to use the gifts; people
need to be set free and healed. But He is more than the
gifts. He is a Person. He is our friend. If we have *Him*, He
is going to come in and shake the Church. He is going to
shake everything in our lives, too. He will bring a refiner's
fire because His job is to nurture and to heal and to get the
Bride ready.

So He comes in and deals with the dross—the bitterness
and pain and resentment in our lives. He opens powerful
doorways of understanding; the Word of God goes from
logos to *rhema*. He awakens our hearts and we begin to long
for deeper places. How can we move through the wilder-
nesses of the earth with any kind of forerunner anointing
unless we have that intimate relationship with the Holy
Spirit? He wants us to get revelation about where we are
going—and revelation of who Jesus is. That is His job. He
wants the Bride to love the Son intimately. We are often
taught in churches that John the Baptist is the best man for
the Bridegroom, but, no, it is the Holy Spirit. He wants to
make the Bridegroom's joy complete.

Some of us have never really known the Holy Spirit as a
Person, as the best friend of the Bridegroom. If we do not
know Him in this way, then unless we are in a season of
renewal or attending meetings where the fire is released,
we feel alone and abandoned. That is because we do not
understand the bridal partnership: The best man is bringing us to the Bridegroom King.

This is a call to bridal intimacy. Cry out for the Holy
Spirit to come. Tell Him you want to know Him person-

ally. "Holy Spirit, we want more of You. We ask You to break our mind-sets where we have limited You. We want to know the best friend of the Bridegroom. We want to be escorted on the marriage chariot through the wilderness to our King."

Psalm 45 gives us this beautiful description of Jesus:

> Your throne, O God, is forever and ever; a scepter of righteousness is the scepter of Your kingdom. You love righteousness and hate wickedness; therefore God, Your God, has anointed You with the oil of gladness more than Your companions. All Your garments are scented with myrrh and aloes and cassia, out of the ivory palaces, by which they have made You glad. Kings' daughters are among Your honorable women; at Your right hand stands the queen in gold from Ophir.
>
> Psalm 45:6–9

In the wedding song of Solomon, we also see Him:

> Who is this coming out of the wilderness like pillars of smoke, perfumed with myrrh and frankincense, with all the merchant's fragrant powders? Behold, it is Solomon's couch, with sixty valiant men around it, of the valiant of Israel. They all hold swords, being expert in war. Every man has his sword on his thigh because of fear in the night. Of the wood of Lebanon Solomon the King made himself a palanquin: He made its pillars of silver, its support of gold, its seat of purple, its interior paved with love by the daughters of Jerusalem. Go forth, O daughters of Zion, and see King Solomon with the crown with which his mother crowned him on the day of his wedding, the day of the gladness of his heart.
>
> Song of Solomon 3:6–11

Jesus, the Bridegroom King, comes out of the ivory palaces. He is clothed in fragrances of myrrh, aloes and cassia.

The perfumes of heaven cling to Him when He comes to earth. He goes into the wilderness of the fallen world with the intent of His heart to get a Bride.

As He emerges from the wilderness of death into resurrection power, we are given this image of Him in the verses above: "Who is this coming out of the wilderness like pillars of smoke, perfumed with myrrh and frankincense?" He is perfumed with myrrh, which signifies that He gave His life for her. Frankincense represents His ongoing intercession for her. He shouts with joy, "Father, I did it! I paid the price. It is finished. My Bride is Mine."

What a picture! It is as though we can see the smoking glory, this fire of God moving around the Son of God. The angels are thrilled. They watch Him as He ascends in pillars of fire back up to the palaces. This is our Jesus. This smoky, fiery, perfumed God! This God who died for His Bride.

The Father says to the Son, "Sit here by Me, on My right hand. Now I must send My Holy Spirit." The most important assignment of the Holy Spirit is to search through the wilderness for the Bride and to get her ready for the One who gave His life for her.

To help us understand how our hearts are awakened to this passionate love, the Father has given us a beautiful parallel in Scripture. It is the story of how Abraham's servant was sent in search of a bride for Isaac, the son of promise.

The Search for a Bride

Genesis 24:1–7 begins the story. Abraham commissioned his servant to find a bride for his son and bring her to him:

> Now Abraham was old, well advanced in age; and the LORD had blessed Abraham in all things. So Abraham said to the oldest servant of his house, who ruled over all that he had,

"Please, put your hand under my thigh, and I will make you swear by the Lord, the God of heaven and the God of the earth, that you will not take a wife for my son from the daughters of the Canaanites, among whom I dwell; but you shall go to my country and to my family, and take a wife for my son Isaac."

And the servant said to him, "Perhaps the woman will not be willing to follow me to this land. Must I take your son back to the land from which you came?"

But Abraham said to him, "Beware that you do not take my son back there. The Lord God of heaven, who took me from my father's house and from the land of my family, and who spoke to me and swore to me, saying, 'To your descendants I give this land,' He will send His angel before you, and you shall take a wife for my son from there."

So the servant loaded ten camels with his master's goods, including many gifts for the bride, and made his way through the wilderness. He had enough supplies on the camels not only to last him during his search for the bride, but also to take her back through the wilderness to the son.

One evening he arrived at a well outside a city in Mesopotamia and had the camels kneel down. Here he decided to wait, for it was the time of day when women from the city would come to draw water. The servant then prayed and put out a fleece: "Lord," he said, "have the maiden who not only gives me a drink of water but also offers to water the camels be the one."

He had barely finished speaking when a beautiful young woman appeared.

Rebekah was doing her chores just as she did every day. She walked to the well and filled her pitcher. The servant jumped up, ran to meet her and asked her for a drink. Something quickened in Rebekah's heart and she responded, "Yes, sir. Drink, and I will water your camels also." That was an extravagant gesture. One thirsty camel can drink about thirty gallons of water, so she probably carried about three hundred gallons from the well to the trough that evening.

The servant had put out a divine fleece; all he had asked for was a drink of water. Rebekah did not know at that time that there was a son; all she saw were camels. But it was a prophetic invitation and she said yes. Rebekah had a servant's heart and was willing to be extravagant in her reply.

When the Holy Spirit comes, why do we so often reject His prophetic invitations? We can handle God as the Father and Jesus as the Good Shepherd, but embracing the Holy Spirit starts to get controversial. We are probably afraid of what He will do to us. But even when we welcome the revival fires of God we tend to see the work of the Holy Spirit as just a renewal phenomenon. I think it is wonderful to laugh and be refreshed or weep and intercede for the lost. It is a marvelous thing to shake under the power of God or sit silently as the deep broodings of the Spirit awaken you. But in the midst of all of this, there needs to be a tenderizing and capturing of our hearts for the Bridegroom that goes beyond "shaking and baking"! The outward manifestations have to be connected to the inward journey of the heart.

In other words, the Holy Spirit's purpose is not just to show up so everyone can fall down. It is all about the Son. The servant is coming to capture and awaken our hearts in preparation for the journey home.

After Rebekah watered the camels, the servant gave her gold jewelry and accepted her offer for his entire entourage to lodge at her home. (How would you like to have a teenage daughter invite a crew like that!) She ran back to her house and told her family what had occurred. When her brother Laban saw the gifts his sister had received, he hurried out to meet the servant and also welcomed him.

So the servant told his story about an old man named Abraham and the miracle birth of a son named Isaac. I am sure as little Rebekah sat there, her heart started to warm. She probably thought, *Oh! There's more than camels here. There is a son.* Her family agreed that the Lord had directed their meeting. Rebekah was the bride whom the servant sought. At this, the servant rejoiced and brought out many wonderful and precious gifts for the whole family. Then they ate and fellowshipped all night. They had a great time!

In the morning the servant was ready to leave. The family asked him to stay, but he said that his mission was urgent. "You see, I have to get the bride to the son." So often we want to stay in the bride's house where all the gifts are and keep up the party. We lack revelation of the journey. We do not understand the magnitude of this incredible love story and the extent to which the Son is longing for His Bride. Every time we follow the Holy Spirit a little closer to the Son, love leaps like fire inside His heart.

So they asked Rebekah if she was willing to go. The Holy Spirit seeks a Bride with a voluntary yes in her heart. Jesus wears many crowns, but the one crown we can give to Him is our voluntary love. She said that she was ready to leave life as she knew it and follow the servant.

This is such an encouraging love story because it gives us hope. We do not know how to get through the wilderness to the Son any more than Rebekah knew how to traverse the wilderness to reach Isaac. She had to trust the servant to get her there. We, too, must partner with the Holy Spirit. He is skillful. He knows the terrain.

Tell Us about the Groom

I am sure that as Rebekah was traveling along, she asked many questions about Isaac: "Okay, but what does Isaac look like? Tell me about him."

The servant might have said, "Well, I have known him from the very beginning. He is wonderful. He is beautiful. He is good and kind. . . ."

Rebekah would have listened with her whole heart as the servant went on to describe all the characteristics about her bridegroom that she longed to know.

So what about *your* Bridegroom? You, like Rebekah, are being led through your own wilderness to come face-to-face with the Son of God. What obstacles, like mountains, will you have to scale? What valleys will cause your heart to faint? Will you find the refreshing pools? The Holy Spirit will take you through this wonderful and terrible terrain. And along the way you will learn more about your Bridegroom.

"Okay," you say, "but what does Jesus look like? Tell me about Him."

"Well," the Servant might respond, "I have known Him from the very beginning. He is wonderful. He is beautiful. He is good and kind. He is full of light, full of compassion. When He sees those who are broken, despised and rejected, He goes quickly to pick them up and carry them. He is a great, tender Shepherd."

He might continue with words from the Song of Solomon 5:10–16; 8:5, paraphrased in italics here. *Your Beloved is chief among ten thousand. His head is like the finest gold. He is ruddy, and His locks are wavy and black.* The Son is dazzling and full of light. He is stunning. His leadership, like gold, has gone through the fire and is clean, pure and solid. He is strong. He has discernment.

His eyes are like a dove, discerning with wisdom. He sees your heart. He sees when you cry out to Him. He knows who you are. He loves you passionately.

His cheeks are like a bed of spices. His cheeks are His emotions. His emotions are so diverse that they are like beds of spices. One reason that Jesus is called the Suffering Servant is because He understands your pain. He is a sympathetic

High Priest who knows your wounding. He understands exactly what you are going through.

His hands are like rods of gold. His legs are like pillars of marble. His sovereignty oversees your destiny. He is strong and He knows where He is taking you. He knows the plans that He has for your life. His favor rests on you.

His mouth is most sweet. He is altogether lovely. Even though His eyes are like fire, His heart melts when He looks at you! At times you get just a taste of the love that awakens your heart toward Him. There are no words to express the joy of sweet communion with Him.

Who is this coming up from the wilderness, leaning upon her beloved? the angels are asking. The answer is the Bride—us! We have found our hearts' desire.

We cry out,

> Set me as a seal upon your heart, as a seal upon your arm; for love is as strong as death, jealousy as cruel as the grave; its flames are flames of fire, a most vehement flame. Many waters cannot quench love, nor can the floods drown it.
>
> Song of Solomon 8:6–7

These divine seals come from partnering with Jesus. A seal of love is placed on our hearts. On our arms is a divine seal of authority. They indicate that we are moving in bridal partnership with Him.

When the Holy Spirit comes and brings the fire, it is but a token of the love of Jesus. He is a consuming fire with rivers of fire around His throne. He is a God of fire! He is a God whose eyes are a consuming fire of love for us.

We must never let reproach or misunderstanding keep us away from our relationship with the Person of the Holy Spirit. We cannot any longer hold onto old paradigms that we have seen in churches in the past. There have been many good and powerful moves of God, but the Lord wants us to learn how to partner with the Holy Spirit in the season we are in right now, the end times.

And what about Rebekah? How did her journey end? Genesis 24:63–67 tells us that Isaac was out in the field one evening, meditating. He looked up and saw a caravan of ten camels approaching. Just at that time, Rebekah also lifted her eyes and saw him. When the servant told her who it was, she dismounted from her camel and followed the servant to Isaac's side. The servant told Isaac all the things he had done and presented the one he had brought safely through the wilderness; his mission was complete.

Isaac undoubtedly looked at his beautiful new bride with a smile in his eyes—remember that his name means "laughter"—and "she became his wife, and he loved her" (Genesis 24:78).

5

Desperation and Visitation

When I worship God, the first thing He shows me is the issues of my heart. It is always that way. Before I can go into the Holy of Holies, I first have to stand in the outer court and let Him show me where my life is not right. In a way, it is like being transparent in my spirit before the Lord.

This is a really vulnerable place with Jesus, but I would not want it any other way. I have made a choice because I love Him. Actually I have tried it all the other ways. I have found that if you are not willing to lose your life, you will die. Apathy, boredom, being lukewarm—these are deadly poisons that will compromise destinies.

Desperation in me says, "God, here am I. Test the motives of my heart. Show me what You want to do in me. Show me where I am not trusting You and where I get afraid. Show me where I look at circumstances instead of keeping my eyes on You." And believe me, He always finds something! It is very humbling.

After He cleans me up, I go before Him and ask Him what is on His heart. That opens the way for visitations, which are fresh encounters with God, times when the hand of God comes down and awakens destiny. Many times I just weep because I feel His heart and I love Him. He is not an "it." He is not a power. He is God. I want relationship. I want to be someone He can trust to be His friend.

I also want to be someone He can use to help others find their destinies. God can give us insight for other people's dreams. That is part of an awakened heart: We speak the prophetic; we speak destiny. It is like looking at someone through the eyes of love and offering a love letter, a new script. "Wait a minute," we might say. "The Lord is showing me that you are creative. I see that you are an entrepreneur. A door is going to open for you." Or, "This has been your experience . . . but God has bigger dreams for you. Don't give up." We get glimpses of what the Father has for people. We begin speaking life and help pull people forward.

After walking with the Lord all these years, I have to say that I do not think that the battle with fear ever ends if you are really on the cutting edge with the Lord. There are always those few awkward moments before the oil of the Holy Spirit begins to flow and you move in it. Even to give a simple word or a simple prophecy involves a leap of faith. But the Lord pushes us forward and says, *Trust Me. I will put words in your mouth that you don't have right now. Step out.*

In the Body of Jesus Christ we need to develop what I call "the eye of the eagle." Eagles are, of course, a prophetic symbol. They can ride the winds to great heights, and still discern movement on the desert floor. Do you see the parallel? We need to soar in the heights and have clear vision of what goes on below. We need to be willing to leave our nests and tend to the needy souls God puts in our paths.

If we are obedient, the Lord can redeem our shortsightedness. If we are desperate, He will visit us.

Eye-Opening Words

Let me give you an example. I remember a trip to Jerusalem that the Lord arranged for me sovereignly. I would never have been able to direct the circumstances that got me there. In fact, I doubted the possibility of this trip until I got on the plane.

As I checked into the Christian hostel where I was staying, I met a couple, Charlie and his wife, Gloria, from New York. Charlie was an amazing man. An archeologist with a PhD in the sciences, he was definitely what I call a "left brainer." Gloria was a nurse. We hit it off right away and headed to the old Jewish quarter, where we talked, laughed and had some pizza. We moved along slowly because Charlie had a great deal of pain in one of his legs from calcium deposits. I discovered that neither of them was a believer. Spirit-filled Jesuit priests from New York had recommended that they stay at the hostel.

A couple of days later, I was walking through the courtyard in the evening on my way to a healing service downtown. My good friend Mahesh Chavda, a seasoned apostle who moves in signs and wonders, was conducting a miracle service, and I was very excited to go. Charlie and Gloria were sitting on the cobblestone patio among the beautiful trees of the courtyard and invited me to join them. I thanked them, but said that I did not have time. I was on my way to a meeting.

Then I felt the Holy Spirit telling me that *this* was my meeting. I began immediately to argue! I told Him that He did not understand. For one thing the meeting in town was for the purpose of ministry, and, for another, I wanted to surprise my friend. This inner conversation with the Holy Spirit happened at the same time that I was talking with Charlie and Gloria.

It grew later and I really wanted to be on my way downtown to the wonderful service! I continued wrestling with the Holy Spirit. Again He said to me, *No. This is your meeting.* Sighing, I finally gave in to the Holy Spirit and told Charlie and Gloria that I would sit for a few minutes.

They told me that they had gone to the fortress Masada that day and wanted me to know that I had been on their minds. I gradually changed the subject and told them that we have a God who has each of us on His mind. To illustrate this, I told them this story about an incident that had occurred just a month before in New Zealand.

I had been getting a manicure, and the young woman doing my nails had expressed interest in my being a minister. The Lord spoke words in my heart, and I gave them to her. I told her how she had loved the Lord as a little girl, but had begun to question the Church and had left Him. I told her that she needed to stop living with her boyfriend and get help for her drug addiction. The Lord also showed me that she had suffered as a child from a sexually abusive father. Then I spoke her dream: "God's desire is for you to be married and have children. But you need to leave this man so that God can heal your life."

Charlie and Gloria listened intently as I explained that the young woman had confirmed the words I had spoken. She had said that she was too afraid to make any changes at that moment, but I knew that the Lord had gotten her attention.

When Charlie spoke, his reaction to this story surprised me. He looked at me and said, "Do you have a word for me?"

I stared back and said, "What?"

Gloria said, "I want one, too."

I shook my head with a laugh. "Wait a minute. You two don't even believe in Him!"

I could practically feel the Lord tapping on my shoulder. *Hello, Jill? These words are for the unsaved, too, you know!*

"Charlie," I said, "do you really want a word?" He nodded. At that moment, I did not have a thing. I had simply shared the story about the young woman to stir their faith. I had no idea that they would want a word. So I sat there, waved my hand toward heaven, literally, and said, "Lord, do You have a word for Charlie and Gloria?"

I looked at Charlie and said, "Oh, Charlie. You have a spirit of death and an afflicting spirit. You are going to die. You have a terminal disease. Your bones are fusing together down your neck and spine, and you don't have long to live."

Charlie's mouth dropped open. He looked at Gloria and said, "How did she do that? That's right!"

I continued speaking the words the Lord was giving me. "People are trying to kill you."

"Yes," he said, "the Greek Mafia."

The Lord gave me more words. I told him that I saw that he had received a blow to the left side of his head. And when he was born, there had been a lot of difficulties.

Gloria jumped in and said, "That's not true."

I said, "Yes, he had a lot of trouble when he was being born. He almost died. As a small child he hung in the balance between life and death."

Charlie looked at his wife and said, "Oh, Gloria, it is true. I never told you that."

Then I looked at Gloria and said, "Gloria, you want to divorce Charlie." Now *her* mouth dropped open, and she began to cry. I said, "Gloria, because you are a nurse and you understand how sick your husband is, you don't think you are going to be able to watch him die. So you have begun to close down your heart. You also want to have children, but have not been able to."

Charlie put his arms around Gloria, but his scientific brain was still whirling. He asked me how I knew all this. I told them that Jesus loved them and that was the only reason He gave me the information. "Charlie, He knew you when you were in your mother's womb. He saw how the enemy wanted to destroy you. He has seen all the assignments of death and the curses on your life and how you are fighting for your life now. Jesus wouldn't give me this information if He didn't want you to accept Him as Lord and Savior."

Then I spoke again to Gloria. "The Lord showed me the secrets of your heart—wanting to divorce Charlie, shutting down your heart, being unable to have children. The Lord loves you. Do you want to accept Him?"

Gloria was sobbing and said, "Yes, I do." She repented and accepted Jesus.

Intellectual Charlie was still not so sure. He said he would consider Jesus as an option.

It was now 9:30 P.M. I thought again of the meeting, but this time with a different purpose. I told them they needed to come with me to the service because they both needed miracles.

We hailed a taxi and arrived at the end of the service. The room was packed with people lined up around the walls. We stood in the back, listening as Mahesh gave prophetic words to those in the audience.

Charlie whispered to me, "Well, if he even guesses what I have, it will be a miracle because only two hundred people in the whole world have my disease."

"Well, excuse me, Charlie, as if God isn't omniscient!" I said. I was laughing. "You don't think God can identify your disease?"

About the third word Mahesh spoke was this: "There is someone here with a spine that is deteriorating and who is going to die. There are also women here who can't have children." Charlie and Gloria both went forward.

After they received prayer from Mahesh, they decided to go back to the hostel. I told them I would meet them in thirty minutes. When I arrived, Charlie was in a tiny office with twenty other people. He was sitting in a chair, rolling up a pant leg. Then he yelled, "I'm healed! I'm healed!

The calcium deposits are gone. I can't believe it. How did it happen? I didn't even feel anything."

I said, "Charlie, it was Jesus. Remember, *in the name of Jesus*? Jesus loves you so much He died for you. That is why He healed your leg." Charlie started running up and down the stairs.

Earlier that evening I had told him that going to Masada was probably his last archeological trip because it was getting so painful for him to walk. He had told me that I was right; he could not even ride his bike anymore. For Charlie to be running up and down the stairs was a miracle. A few days later, after he received many other words, Charlie accepted Jesus as his Savior. His testimony affected all the people who were staying in the hostel. They knew that God had performed a miracle on a man who was dying.

When you feel loved, anything is attainable. Your dreams are attainable. The world is attainable. God is already offering us the love we desire, but we have to be desperate. When we want Him more than anything else, His love infuses life into our homes, our businesses, our relationships. Love inspires. When we can truly say, "I am worthy of that love, no matter what I have done or have not done," then God can come in big ways and visitations happen.

That is really the key to all we desire. Do we want to move in signs and wonders? The key is in the heart of love. If we feel what He feels, our hearts are awakened. We love what He loves.

Then we begin to see people differently. We look past their job descriptions or titles and think, *How does this person really feel? How does she think? What does he see? Can I come alongside her? Can I love him? Can I be her friend?* We then move into the heart of a loving God, which opens us to greater love for each other. Destiny is awakened when we go into the heart of Jesus.

Often I sense the Holy Spirit pouring hot "oil" into golden menorahs that represent individuals, ministries and churches.

He sets them on fire. My desire is to partner with Him and be one of His fire starters. I want to help equip the Body. I want to see people praying and doing the works of Jesus. I want to continue to give it away so that He will keep giving more of Himself to me. It is like the alabaster box that was broken over Him: The fragrance of the perfume filled the entire room. I want to be willing to let the Lord break me so that my fragrance will fill the entire room.

What makes each man or woman desperate for God? So often it seems that we run to God only when tragedy hits. Suddenly we plug in and say, "O God! O God! I am listening. I want You!" But how do we get to the place where that hunger starts to become a lifestyle?

When I think of this kind of driving spirit, I think of Moses. Even though he was already set apart, even though God had already visited him, it *still* was not enough. He wanted more.

Moses and God Meet Face-to-Face

Moses was set apart even as a child. His story begins in the second chapter of Exodus. The Bible says that when Pharaoh became fearful of the growing number of Jewish people in Egypt, he commanded that all of their newborn males were to be put to death. Hoping to save the infant's life, Moses' mother set him afloat in a basket in the river. Miraculously, he was picked up by the daughter of Pharaoh, who took him as her own. Other than those early months in his childhood home, Moses was raised as an Egyptian prince.

When he was forty years old, Moses felt compassion for his Hebrew brothers in slavery. He tried to work it out his own way and wound up murdering someone. He then had to run for his life and spent the next forty years in the wilderness.

At eighty years of age, when he felt he could not talk well and that there was no purpose to his life at all, God met him. Moses did not receive his calling when he was a young, proud prince but when he was an old man aware of his frailty.

Why did God choose Moses to lead His people out of Egypt? Moses knew the ways of the palace as well as the language and the ways of the people. But there was something else about Moses: He was desperate for intimacy with God. Look at this description of his meeting with God on Mount Sinai during the early wilderness travels:

> Then it came to pass on the third day, in the morning, that there were thunderings and lightnings, and a thick cloud on the mountain; and the sound of the trumpet was very loud, so that all the people who were in the camp trembled. And Moses brought the people out of the camp to meet with God, and they stood at the foot of the mountain. Now Mount Sinai was completely in smoke, because the LORD descended upon it in fire. Its smoke ascended like the smoke of a furnace, and the whole mountain quaked greatly. And when the blast of the trumpet sounded long and became louder and louder, Moses spoke, and God answered him by voice. Then the LORD came down upon Mount Sinai, on the top of the mountain. And the LORD called Moses to the top of the mountain, and Moses went up.
>
> Exodus 19:16–20

Moses met with God, and they were intimate friends. How many of us would like that kind of intimacy with Jesus? It is in the place of deep broodings that God gives us His secrets and mysteries.

The Intercessor Seeks an Answer

Exodus 24–35 tells the familiar yet extraordinary story of Moses. After the incredible "mountaintop" experience on Mount Sinai of having a forty-day visitation, receiving the Ten Commandments and having God inscribe the Law on his heart, Moses was ready to go back down the mountain when the Lord, in His anger, spoke about what was happening in the camp below.

The people had gotten restless. They were probably bored and wondered what had happened to Moses. So they built a golden calf and began to worship it as the god that had taken them out of bondage in Egypt. They were involved in sexual perversion and idolatry. The Lord's jealousy burned as He told Moses what was happening and how He planned to consume those "stiff-necked people" (Exodus 32:9) and make a great nation from Moses' descendants instead.

' But Moses pleaded with God to relent. He was an intercessor who stood in the gap as a deliverer and pleaded for their lives. "Oh, God, don't kill them! What would the Egyptians say? Would they say that You took Your people out of Egypt to destroy them? It would give You a bad reputation, God. And after all, You promised that the descendants of Abraham, Isaac and Jacob would inherit the Promised Land." Moses, like a true lover, was more concerned with God's reputation than his own pleasure.

When Moses returned to camp and saw that the people were in full rebellion, he threw down the tablets and called out for those who were on the Lord's side to stand beside him. The Levites joined Moses with their swords in their hands. At his word, they killed three thousand people that day. Moses could have quit; it would have been a really good time. Instead he pitched his tent outside the camp as a Tabernacle of meeting with God.

' In desperation, Moses cried out for a greater encounter with the Lord—he needed a deeper visitation. It was not enough to see a bush ablaze or watch the Red Sea part or even to see supernatural provision each day with the raining down of manna. He cried out for more. He wanted to see God's face, and he would not take no for an answer. Total desperation, unquenchable hunger and unswerving commitment to his people caused Moses to contend with God for His presence.

When facing enormous trials, Moses chose to press into God with greater desperation. Do your difficulties cause you to run *to* God or *from* God? No matter what your circumstances, God is inviting you to come up higher out of the valley of death and destroyed dreams. He will give you the wings of an eagle to soar up the mountain to greater heights in Him.

Are you willing to find your own tent of meeting and cry out for another visitation as Moses did? Is discouragement driving you into the face of God? Will you climb the mountain of God again?

The Glory Comes!

Now whenever Moses entered the Tabernacle, the pillar of cloud would descend and stand at the Tabernacle door. "The LORD spoke to Moses face to face, as a man speaks to his friend" (Exodus 33:11). So after the extraordinary visitation on the mountain and the purging of the camp, Moses went into the Tabernacle and cried out, "God, I need more of You. I don't have enough. Show me Your glory."

The Lord said, "But Moses, you have more than any man on earth."

Moses responded, "No, I need to know that Your presence is with me. I need to know You. I need to see You. We cannot go ahead unless I know that You are with us. I must see Your glory."

God said, "Moses, I am with you. You have My presence and My favor."

But Moses persisted. "Lord, that is not enough. I can't go on if I don't see You." What a picture of the lover crying out for intimacy with the beloved!

So God agreed. "But," He said, "I am going to hide you in the cleft of a rock, for if you should actually see My face you would die." As Moses was hidden safely in the cleft of the rock, the Bible says that all the goodness of God passed in front of him (see Exodus 33:19).

After this the Lord told Moses to return to Mount Sinai. While Moses was up there fasting and praying for another forty days, the Ten Commandments were chiseled out on stones once again. As the Lord proclaimed more revelations and more mysteries, Moses bowed and worshiped.

When Moses came down the mountain and spoke with the people, he was so full of the glory of the Lord that he had to cover his face with a veil. But when he went back to the Tabernacle, he took the veil off because he was meeting with the Lord—as if to say, "Hello, my friend!"

Moses was desperate, then he experienced a visitation. Are we willing, when we go through those times of being challenged with death, hopelessness, confusion and assaults of the enemy, to tell the Lord that we are hungry for more of Him? That we love Him passionately?

If we go to Him, He will give us His heart. This is why we were created: *We were created because God wanted relationship. And as we are in relationship with Him, we can see others through His eyes.*

The whole world is crying out. People need encounters that are not framed in religion, which is dead, but in *relationship.* God wants to move with His presence in a fresh way. He wants to release an outpouring of divine visitations such as the earth has never seen.

The move of God is not power; the move of God is the presence of Jesus Christ.

92

The Heart of Jesus

One time when I was in prayer, the Lord gave me much deeper revelation and understanding of this. It was an amazing visitation that happened to me during one of my own Master Potter conferences.

I found myself moving at breakneck speed through a realm of eternity in heaven. It was smoky all around me, like swirling glory. As I looked below, I could see glimpses of a sea of glass and hear sounds of worship.

In front of me, huge gates opened, and I went through them. I was astounded as I found myself close up against the chest of Jesus. I could feel His robe underneath my face; it felt like linen. I could hear His gigantic heart beating and beating. Then I could feel the arms of the Lord around me, holding me and loving me. I felt so secure and so protected. There was no other place anywhere in the world that I wanted to be more than there—leaning on my Beloved, snuggled up against His chest, feeling His arms around me and hearing His heart.

Then the most amazing thing happened. It was as if the robe against my face disappeared and His heart opened up. I went into a mysterious realm and slipped into His heart. One moment I was like John the Beloved leaning on the Lord's chest; the next moment I was inside one of the chambers of His heart.

It seemed as if the chamber was made of flesh—it felt very vulnerable—and I could feel the loud pounding of eternity. Then I realized that I was hearing the cries of the oppressed and broken and lost as they surrounded me. I could also hear Him weeping. This great Intercessor was weeping for the lost. His heart was like a wall and inscribed on it were the names of every single human being on earth. He was crying out for each one of these names. Each one. If I looked at a name, his or her face appeared and I had a glimpse into that person's life. It was like experiencing heaven's wailing wall.

I could feel as well as hear the people in this wall crying out: "Is there a God? Is He really there? Do You feel my pain?" In the enormous chamber of His heart, I could hear all of humanity, every name, every face and every circumstance. I could hear the sounds of the abused and the broken: "Is there really a God?" I could also hear the prayers of the intercessors on earth and the cries of the lost. Then it was as if, underneath, I could hear the sound of the blood of the martyrs, "How long, O Lord? How long, O Lord?"

The response of His great pain for each suffering person was like a heart attack.

Gradually I realized that I could hear music and other sounds of heaven. I remember the words *Holy is the Lamb*. All of the voices and instruments were mingled, as if an enormous orchestra and choir were assembled in the weeping heart of the Lord. It made a great crescendo—the anguish of the people and the music of heaven in the midst of His great intercession.

Then I felt as if the Lord was speaking to me. *The key to apostolic authority is love. If people want to move in signs and wonders and miracles, if they want to see heaven breaking in to take whole territories, then they need to discover My heart and My compassion. Then I will give them the power to set the captives free and the anointing to see the sick healed and the dead raised.*

In the distance I could see other chambers, like other rooms in heaven. His heart was like heaven itself with many different dimensions. I could see the throne ahead but my attention was given to His words: *If people want to move in My power and My presence, they need to have My love and My heart.*

Intimacy with God

God is asking, "Do you want a visitation? Are you willing to ask Me to come and meet you where you live?"

It is wrong to think that the only place God will move is in a church or a conference setting. Those places might be compared to a big living room or a banquet hall. But the Lord may also meet with us in the rose garden, in the library or at a poolside family gathering. I simply mean, of course, that we can share times of deep intimacy with God in the course of daily living. He takes us into the deep places of His heart so that compassion will move from our heads to our own hearts.

Visitations can last just a few minutes or days and days. It all depends upon the sovereignty of God; we cannot make them happen. But He honors the desire in us that says, "Lord, give me desperation for You that nothing else will satisfy." The timetable is up to Him.

One amazing thing about visitations is that they move us farther into holiness. Many times when God comes in a visitation, we are like Isaiah, who cried out that he was a man of unclean lips. When we see what is really in us, we repent.

One of my constant prayers is for hunger, but I cannot give you my hunger. Each one of us has choices to make, such as whether or not we will open our hearts when we feel His nudges and touches. It is up to each of us to ask Him for more.

Are you willing to focus on your first love? Are you willing to be on the cutting edge? Do you want to be a long-distance runner? Are you saying, "O God, I want to go for the gold"?

6

The Price behind the Anointing

We see that lovers do not always take the easy road.
When you pursue Jesus it becomes addictive; you get ruined. You just want more of Him. He becomes your closest confidant. He starts to move around you wherever you go. You can hardly wait to be with Him. It is not a question of discipline; you just want Him all the time. You weep with Him; He weeps with you. You go deeper and deeper into divine intimacy.

No true romantic needs a handbook—lovers follow their hearts. But I have found that a few keys help to unlock this divine romance. After I share these with you, I want to look at the life of one more lover. Her story is a summation of treks through desperation and visitation. It also shows us the cost of being a lover and the joy of fulfilled destiny. It is the story of Mary, the mother of Jesus.

First, here are five ancient keys for lovers.

1. Touch Heaven through Worship

During worship there is a great deal happening in the supernatural. This is when the creative presence of the Lord touches His people. Some see pictures, hear Scriptures, get words of knowledge or hear His voice. What does worship do? Worship changes the heart of man and moves the heart of God. It takes only a few seconds of a face-to-face encounter with the manifest presence of God to change the course of history for you, your city or your nation.

In the Old Testament His presence is often referred to as the Shekinah glory, the fire of divine visitation. Second Chronicles 5:14, for instance, tells the story of God's glory filling the Temple. The priests could not stand in that glory. The thick weight of God's presence settled in so heavily that the people could only lie prostrate before Him.

Worship is the way we encounter Him. It is an invitation to go beyond the boundary lines in heaven where God will whisper the secrets of His burning heart. We can hear the love songs of God's heart and sing them back to Him.

2. Commune with God through Prayer

Many Christians struggle because they feel that their intercession is mostly empty cries to an invisible God who seems far away. We think that our prayers shoot only as high as the ceiling and then bounce back, unheard and unanswered. But God loves spending intimate time alone with us. He promises that He will hear and answer. "Call to Me, and I will answer you, and show you great and mighty things" (Jeremiah 33:3).

Communing with God is, in fact, the highest purpose for lovers. Our hunger for God Himself is what fuels our prayer lives. When being in His presence is our main goal, we can approach the throne of God with the confidence that He loves to meet with us. As John Bunyan said, "In prayer it is better to have a heart without words than words without a heart."

We sometimes forget that listening is part of prayer. Any intimate relationship involves being a good listener in order to share on a deeper level. God listens to us, but how many of us stop to listen to Him? How can we know His heart when we do all of the talking?

The goal in prayer is not to have our prayers answered, but to encounter God Himself. Fellowship and intimacy are not based upon the hours we spend in prayer. Rather, intimacy comes as we spend time with God all through the day. Prayer should not consist solely of storming the gates of heaven with a list of requests. That can quickly become an empty exercise of words. Our prayers must be desperate cries from our hearts for encounters with His heart.

Having an audience with God is not something to take lightly. It is an incredible honor to rest in the knowledge that the omnipotent God of the universe has one joy above all else—to spend time with us.

3. Wear Garments of Humility

The Holy Spirit is training us in humility to rule and reign with Jesus as His Bride. If we are to be yoked to the Bridegroom, we must wear the same wedding garments He wore. Jesus, the King of kings, chose a crown of thorns. How much more should we adorn ourselves in the beauty of meekness? He forsook His divine robes of righteousness for earthly homespun robes. How much more should we cover ourselves with a mantle of humility?

At the Marriage Supper of the Lamb, each one of us will be wrapped in brilliant garments reflecting the fruits and rewards of our earthly lives. Stunning, tailor-made, royal robes will be our portion. During our time on earth, however, it is as if our outer garments are simple burlap robes. Underneath are the beautiful fabrics of our gifting. Sometimes the Lord displays these openly, but generally they remain a secret testimony between Him and us.

The goal is to be so accepted and confident in the Light of the world that we do not need the limelight. At the end of the day, His opinion is the only one that counts. When we are rooted and grounded in His affections, it is easier not to care about promoting ourselves. It is then that we find ourselves in that wonderful place of reckless abandonment—of being a true lover of Jesus.

4. Let Him Lead the Dance

When I started Master Potter Ministries years ago, I gave dramatic presentations as a performing arts ministry. I have mentioned in chapter 1 how I began by making pots for children in a rainy field. Well, after that I began to set up the wheel onstage along with musicians, singers and actors. We presented prophetic dramas dealing with real-life issues.

It was a new and controversial approach because I portrayed God and yet I was a woman. Every once in a while, a pastor would ask, "How can you be a woman and play God?" Even though God touched people in the performances, I wrestled with this question because I certainly was not trying to make a statement about feminism.

One day I asked the Lord about this. "Lord," I said, "how can You have me, as a woman, portray You?"

He asked a question back: *What would you have God look like?*

"Well," I replied, "a craggy old potter, olive skin, bald head, long beard. Kind of like Father Abraham."

I felt His laughter. He said, *Jill, it's obvious that you're not a man and that you represent My heart and voice to the people. Because you are a woman, no one can ever idolize you and say,*

"There's God." So everyone can receive from you. This is My wisdom even though it seems upside down to you.

His wisdom was far different from mine, of course. When I realized that I was just a symbol of God's heart and that I was not trying to play Him, then I was fine. It had felt as though I was out of order, but I was really in His divine order.

God is asking all of us to be flexible and to let Him be God. We offend Him when we try to control Him through our understanding of "religion." We say, "Let everything be done in decency and order," but there is something greater than our human, logical order: He has *divine order*. Divine order was for Jesus to spit on the ground and make mud and spread it on a man's eyes so that he would be healed (see John 9:6). That does not sound too orderly!

Are we willing to move in His divine order, or are we so fenced in by formulas that we miss the move of the Holy Spirit altogether? Are we more consumed with the fame of His name or protecting our reputations? Are we willing to step out of the boat in faith even if we face rejection? What are we willing to risk to learn to hear the Lord? We need to be willing to do anything for God—even make mistakes.

We must make a covenant to be available for any way God wants to use us. In my journey of being a weak and broken earthenware vessel, I purposed in my heart not just to fall back on religious tools and rituals that I could pull out of a bag of ministry tricks. Rather, I chose to be willing to be a fool for Jesus. When we do not understand the dance steps, we follow His lead simply because we love Him.

5. Let Adversity Press You into Intimacy

Seventy-five percent of all Christians live in Third World nations—nations that are predominantly Hindu, Buddhist and Muslim. More than six hundred million Christians live as second-class citizens in these societies. Persecution in many nations means extortion, family division or excommunication, harassment, discrimination in employment and education, and even death.

Here is just one instance that happened several years ago but has stayed in my heart. A young woman from Sudan, Africa, was severely beaten and raped by Muslims simply because she was wearing a cross. When she tried to escape, they slit her throat and rammed a bayonet in her back. She survived the brutal assault and became pregnant. She is now raising her child.

In the Western Church today, the thought of intimacy with Jesus too often echoes in church halls as a lovely sentiment but not a life-and-death decision. These institutions relate the desire for intimacy to Philippians 3:10: "That I may know Him and the power of His resurrection." Usually, though, they do not finish the verse. It goes: "and the fellowship of His sufferings, being conformed to His death."

In this irony is a powerful revelation—intimacy comes through suffering. That is why the Holy Spirit chose to use Paul not only to pen these words but also to demonstrate them through his own life by suffering for the Gospel.

We must not accept the pacifying theology that suffering is outside the will of God, or that suffering is a sign of Satan having his way in a believer's life. Accusations in our hearts about God's unwillingness to alleviate pain and suffering will prevent us from embracing the cross. If we truly want to be a Bride fit for her Bridegroom, we must be willing to do what He did for us: lay down our lives for the sake of love (see Revelation 12:10–11).

This takes us to the life of one who knew great joy in Jesus' presence and yet experienced great suffering as she watched her hopes and dreams seem to crumble. Mary, Jesus' mother, shows us how God shares divine intimacy with the heart that loves Him.

Mary's Dance of Love

So often we think of Mary only as the gentle teenaged girl of the Christmas story, but there is so much more. We need to look at the tapestry of her whole life. She is the only person in the Word of God who is introduced before the life of Jesus, who is with Him all through His ministry, whose future earthly care Jesus ensures from the cross and who is in the Upper Room when the Church is born at Pentecost.

Mary shows us how our prophetic journeys with God are cyclical. We have seasons that encompass great visitations, spiritual warfare leading to the wilderness, ordinary life and times of ministry that take us to the cross. This leads to resurrection, making us carriers of the glory. Then the cycle begins again.

Radical Visitation

One night the angel Gabriel came to me. Me, can you imagine? A Jewish girl living in poverty in the little town of Nazareth. What did I have to offer anyone, especially almighty God?

His voice filled my whole room; I was terrified. He told me not to fear and that I would give birth to the Messiah. I cried out, "Yes, let it be unto me according to Your word."

The Holy Spirit overshadowed Mary. A radical impartation of the fiery seed of the Father pierced her womb and impregnated her with Jesus. This ushered in the Messianic age through the One who was the fulfillment of all the Old Testament prophecies and the Law.

Mary possessed a heart of devotion and childlike faith. She was a vessel chosen to be the mother of Jesus, yet the Bible never indicates that she moved in miracles. She simply said, "Yes, let it be done unto me," and it changed her life forever. That is why we can all be like Mary. We can

103

all embrace a life of prayer, purity and humility. We can all cry out to be overshadowed by the Holy Spirit to bring revival, to be impregnated with His purposes.

But there is a price behind the anointing. Like human births, birthing the things of the Spirit can be painful—and messy. Revival is not always neat and tidy, either. It can be controversial, and stigma is often associated with it. It can be dangerous because Jesus is revival, and He will always shake systems.

Why did King Herod feel so threatened by a little baby wrapped in swaddling cloths tucked in a manger in Bethlehem? We must realize that this was much more than an enemy persecuting the Jews in the natural. When Jesus was born, heaven invaded earth: War was declared.

Herod's actions paralleled a supernatural confrontation. When the Kingdom of God broke forth on earth, Satan retaliated with demonic fury in order to kill Jesus before He could fulfill the will of the Father.

Spiritual Warfare

In the middle of the night Joseph shook me awake. He was terrified, explaining something about Herod wanting Jesus dead and us leaving town—now. He grabbed Jesus, and we were out the door before I could even understand. In just a matter of minutes we were embarking on another journey—no explanations, no good-byes. I looked back at our lodgings in Bethlehem as we slipped into the night.

Satan often goes after the move of God in its infancy, when it is most vulnerable. God told Joseph to take the Child and His mother and flee from Herod's slaughtering army. They were given a divine strategy and were hidden in the enemy's camp: Egypt.

The stirrings of revival rouse the demonic realm. Thus, the greater your call and destiny, the greater the spiritual warfare. The enemy wants to abort your prophetic promises.

Why Egypt? Why pagan Egypt? It is the land of bondage for our people. Moses led us out. Will we die there like our forefathers? We live as refugees. I keep wondering why God didn't just remove Herod.

How many times have you been given powerful prophetic words when the Lord says, *You will be in front of kings and this will happen and that will happen.* But He does not tell you that perhaps the king is not born yet and it will be another thirty years before the fulfillment of that call. Instead of going from A to B you find yourself going from A to M. You are heading for Egypt.

Ordinary Life

Finally God spoke to Joseph in another dream. Once again he shook me awake, telling me excitedly about Herod's death. This time it was me who grabbed Jesus and ran out the door! We could not get home fast enough.

Things eventually settled down. Joseph set up his carpenter shop and we had more children.

Mothering Jesus is so challenging. When He was twelve, we were returning from Jerusalem in a large group and I realized Jesus wasn't playing with the other children. We returned, frantic. I cried all day as we searched from first light until dark, then I prayed all night. This went on for three days. Finally we found Him in the Temple. His explanation was that I should have known He was there. Oy vey! I wanted to ground Him until He was 21.

Are you hidden and living an ordinary life? Punching a clock, changing diapers, making car payments while crying out, "Lord, have You forgotten me? Why don't people recognize my gifting? Don't they realize I had a radical visitation back in 1992?"

105

Mary had three decades of obscurity to develop a hidden testimony—a secret history with God. For us, it is a time to build family, community and greater intimacy with Jesus. But every once in a while, we cry out in desperation, "I'm tired of waiting. Have You forgotten about me?" This is a season of preparation where God works patience, passion and devotion.

Finally, Ministry Begins

When I was in my mid-forties, life changed dramatically for our family. Jesus started bringing home a ragtag bunch of friends to dinner. He never could resist a stray. Then we were at a wedding, and He changed water to wine. Now He is moving in signs and wonders. In the blink of an eye He has a huge crowd following Him everywhere. It has been a long time coming, but I can see now that with this popularity, He will soon be King of the Jews. The excitement of the crowds grows daily as Jesus walks among the people, bringing revival. But what does He mean, "Who is My mother?"

Mary had to relinquish control even in the midst of an outpouring of the Spirit. In our lives and ministries, we also have to let go. Just as Jesus accepted the cup from His Father's hand, we also have to relinquish our own will and follow, even if it takes our lives to the cross. And it will.

The Dark Night of the Soul

My Son! Why didn't You defend Yourself? You confounded the priests when You were twelve years old. Why didn't You speak to these men? Why did You let them condemn You to death?

I have seen the raw power of God move through You—demons flee, blind eyes open, lepers are cleansed. Thousands have been healed by Your word. You could have commanded angels to save You. You were going to be King of the Jews! It was prophesied.

I didn't make this up. The angel Gabriel visited me; it all happened as he said. It wasn't supposed to end like this.

Why, God, why? Why have You forsaken Him? Why have You forsaken me? He was supposed to deliver all of us. He was our salvation, and now He is gone. If You really love us, why would You allow this?

Mary's anguished heart bled under the shadow of a Roman cross. She had no revelation of the resurrection. She could not see the demonic powers raging against Jesus, or the sins of the world crushing Him. Nor could she see as Jesus, the mighty warrior, snatched the keys of death and hell by the power of His shed blood. All she knew was that after waiting for 33 years, with Jesus in the prime of His life, everything was dying—not only her precious Son, but every prophetic promise she had clung to: Gabriel's stunning announcement, Elizabeth's confirmation, angelic choirs serenading country shepherds, the Magi's trek from the East bringing gifts, Anna's and Simeon's testimonies at the Temple. She watched it all die with His shattered body at Golgotha.

When Jesus chose to go to the cross, Mary was compelled by love to be there, too. We want to believe the Lord will rescue us at the last moment, but often His plan is to crucify us. Everything dies at the cross: our relationships, ministries, agendas, reputations, finances.

As we hit bottom, we hear the tormenting voice of the enemy whispering, "Your life is almost over and you have nothing to show for it. Where is your God now?" But as God takes us through these hot, purifying fires, He works gold in the depth of our being. He gives us love that cannot be quenched by circumstances. The challenge is to believe in the goodness of God.

If we cry out to be part of the Bride, then we need to be identified with the sufferings of the cross. In the midst of great agony and pain, when no one is there, Jesus holds us. A deeper intimacy of bridal love takes place as we cling to Him during times of suffering. We all need to cry out in total surrender, "Lord, I've nowhere else to go. You are my all in all."

Resurrection!

He's alive! He is risen! When I heard those words, my heart nearly burst. I ran to see for myself. I thought I'd cried all my tears on Golgotha, but when our eyes met, it was like a flood. As I ran into His open arms, He scooped me up and spun me around with joyous laughter.

Those times we shared were the most precious of my life. They made it easier to release Him—again. As I watched Him ascend, I prayed familiar words: "Lord, be it unto me as You will, for the rest of my life."

Out of great death comes great life! Mary's prophetic promises were no doubt limited by her worldview. She would have seen Jesus as King over the little nation of Israel during her life. In reality He is King of kings and Lord of lords for all people, for all time. At the cross He crucifies our limited view concerning the fulfillment of our destinies and resurrects it to His eternal view.

Carriers of the Glory

Explosions of glory! The tangible presence of the Holy Spirit! This time it was not just me who was overshadowed but all one hundred twenty of us. Tongues like fire fell, and we were gloriously baptized in the Holy Spirit.

We were so excited. We gave ourselves to prayer night and day, sharing all we had and loving each other so much. We grew from one hundred and twenty to three thousand to five thousand. Signs, wonders and miracles followed as we told everyone about Jesus. It should be easy to grow the Church until we see Jesus coming again in the clouds.

They were baptized in the Holy Spirit, and the Church was set ablaze. They received the gift of tongues and the courage to be radical and passionate lovers of Jesus Christ. The outpouring of the Holy Spirit was, and still is, a ministry of multiplication, intimacy and partnership. When the Holy Spirit moves through us, it is not just for our benefit. He wants to bring conviction, salvation, healing and deliverance to suffering humanity.

Life was anything but easy for Mary and the early Church. Persecution scattered the believers, resulting in the spread of the Gospel to other nations. Mary's journey on earth likely continued through seasons of revival and warfare—cycles of life and death maturing her toward bridal love.

Our passionate, lovesick Bridegroom wants us to be His Bride and love Him wholeheartedly—not just when we finally see Him face-to-face, but throughout this perilous faith-walk on earth. As we peer into the glass darkly, we sometimes see so little of Him that we grow discouraged.

Beloved, never let your heart grow faint. Never give up. We are lovers on a lifelong journey. Let's pray to be overshadowed by His Spirit, impregnated with His purposes and eager to do His will. The journey of the lover's heart is where it all begins and never ends.

Will You Pay the Price?

Imagine that you are sitting in church on a Sunday morning. Did you have to rush to get the kids ready? Did some car cut into your lane and nearly cause you to have a wreck? Did you arrive irritable but put on a "happy face" anyway? Or maybe you are sitting in the pew like a dry piece of wood, wishing something radical would happen.

The worship service begins, and you are amazed to feel the gentle wind of refreshment washing over you. Then very subtly the room fills with a sweet fragrance. The atmosphere around you seems to swirl with colors as you enter a realm outside of time. You breathe deeply, allowing your being to be filled and cleansed with the breath of heaven.

You bask in the wonderful presence of the Holy Spirit. Can you hear the celestial music of the wedding flutes and harps? Can you feel the surges of His fiery devotion sweeping over you? If you could, you would never leave this place of serenity and peace. You sense movement, and as you open your eyes, you experience a vision. The entire church fills with the glory of the Lord and the room transforms into a pottery studio. Each person is a clay vessel in various stages of preparation. Then two extraordinarily beautiful vessels enter the sanctuary.

These vessels exude authority as they simmer and blaze in the supernatural light. They are magnificent vessels full of the Shekinah glory, and their transparent glazes reflect the image of the glorious Son of God. In your spirit you see Jesus, the "Master Potter," enter the room and embrace both vessels warmly. They laugh, sharing mysteries among themselves. Longing stirs in your heart as you witness their special relationship.

You watch as they move among the pews, healing the sick, setting captives free and declaring fiery proclamations from the heart of the Father. You are aware somehow that they paid a high price for their anointing, but the yearning to be like them is powerfully awakened in your heart.

Watching them with obvious delight, Jesus then turns and catches your eye. His unrelenting love beckons to the deepest longing of your heart. The painful neediness of your soul is exposed by His fiery gaze. He is inviting you into a place of greater intimacy. "Will you follow Me?"

The room is again transformed as heavenly portals open, ushering in the glory realm. Swirling gusts of dazzling magnificence surround the Master Potter as He becomes the heavenly Bridegroom. His handsome, rugged face radiates like the sun. His clothing is breathtaking. He walks up and down the aisles, carrying wedding garments over His arms. Your gaze falls on the shimmering fabric. Each garment is different, but all are adorned with pearls, symbolizing the fires ahead for those who choose the fullness of bridal love. Your heart races as He approaches.

Then His passionate gaze locks onto your very being, and you hear His voice: "Beloved, I am calling *you* to fiery bridal love. I am calling you to come into the high fires and allow My glory to engulf you. I long for you to be like the chosen vessels you see here. But there is a price! You have to die to your reputation, your theology and all of your religious formulas. You have to let go of your fears and your control. Do you love Me enough to come, or will you be content to live out your life in the pews of the church?"

His love beckons your heart's deepest longings. And yet you sit quietly for a moment, pondering your answer. This could be dangerous. . . . It could cost you everything—your identity, your friends, perhaps even your life. You are hesitant to say yes, but the thought of remaining in the mundane safety of a church pew no longer seems inviting.

The holiness and purity of His presence drives out fear. Deep passion for the Bridegroom rises within your breast. Your gaze leaves His piercing eyes for a moment and travels to the gossamer wedding garments. Your spirit stirs forcefully within you and your heart cries, "Yes! I am Yours forever."

Part Three

WARRIORS

And from the days of John the Baptist until the present time, the kingdom of heaven has endured violent assault, and violent men seize it by force [as a precious prize—a share in the heavenly kingdom is sought with most ardent zeal and intense exertion].

Matthew 11:12, AMPLIFIED

7

Knowing the Times
and Seasons

This is a season of warfare. Governments are colliding. War games are escalating.

But I am not talking only about the global crises we read and hear about every day. This is an accelerated time in the spiritual realm, as well, and for dreamers and lovers it could not be more exciting. If you have resurrection anointing, the resurrection power living inside of you, then everywhere you go you are dangerous to the enemy. You are part of a radical army carrying out orders of the King of glory.

I believe that we are in a time just like the days before Jesus was born. Angels appeared; people spoke with prophetic voices; prayers for God's presence were answered. He is coming to earth again, this time to set up His Kingdom.

It is a thrilling adventure for the Bride. What spurs us on? The breaking in of the supernatural—the "suddenlies" of God. These experiences inspire us to become holy revolutionaries and see souls won for the Kingdom. All we need is one dream, one visitation. We can be driving down the road and have an open vision. We can be in an elevator, a market, an airplane, and God will work through us. We cannot brag and say it is anything we have done; it is a place of humility. Many times God provides us with prophetic words or visions in order to give us credibility with our hurt and dying world.

Once when I was ministering in Utah, some women from the conference gave me the gift of a massage. As I was enjoying this treat, the young gal who was giving it to me said, "I don't feel very good." I started praying silently in the Spirit, thinking I would give her strength.

All of a sudden she screamed, fell to the floor and began manifesting demonic spirits. I looked over the edge of the table and the Lord gave me a word of knowledge. He told me that her boyfriend was a Satanist and had cursed her. Many more words of freedom followed as I took her through deliverance right there.

When we have God living in our hearts, His presence surrounds us like a force field, moving around us and penetrating darkness wherever we go. The more we walk in deep intimacy with Jesus, the greater the field of His presence. I have read that when nineteenth-century revivalist Maria Woodworth-Etter ministered to people, reports circulated that the presence and power of God touched people sovereignly, miles from where her meetings were being held!

As warriors we have the glory of God coming out of us all the time—even though the glory does not belong to us. That is why the demons in the young woman giving the massage reacted within her. Today this highly educated woman is a powerful prophetic leader in her church and in the marketplace. She is a healer and deliverer of many others.

Dreamers and lovers must press into Jesus as never before. He will take away our fear and teach us new strategies. If Jesus can use me, one of the most unlikely vessels, Jesus can use you. Someone once said that no one's life is wasted; it can always serve as a bad example! That has helped me through my faux pas and fumbling.

As we begin to move in the strategies God lays out before us, windows, or realms, in the heavens will break open, and the government of God will come to earth. Every idol will be knocked over, and any houses built on sand will crumble. These shakings, accompanied by extraordinary signs and wonders, will produce the greatest harvest of souls.

I want to look at three biblical stories that show us how to use fresh words and strategies garnered from the war rooms of heaven. The examples of Deborah, Joshua and Rahab help us understand the call in specific times and seasons. Deborah's and Rahab's stories are particularly important for women, I think, in the sense that women may be more hesitant to seek battle stations even in a spiritual world. But none of us can ignore the prophetic call to evangelism. The fields are white with the harvest. Or, to use an analogy that we will draw on later in this chapter, it is time to go fishing.

Let's see how these Bible figures in turn answer the prophetic call to war, learn to follow divine strategies and show that the most unlikely members of society are desperate for a word from God.

Deborah: Prophetic Call to War

Deborah, a judge and prophetess whose story is told in Judges 4–5, held court under a palm tree between the cities of Ramah and Bethel in the mountains of Ephraim. She was not a judge such as we might see in a county courthouse; she was the executive leader of the entire nation of Israel. She

117

moved governmentally in both civil and spiritual matters, handling civil disputes among the Israelites and speaking prophetic words from the Lord. She was also called "a mother in Israel" (Judges 5:7). The Bible says that Deborah, wife of Lapidoth, arose when the city gates were at war. This was during the time that Israel was being oppressed harshly by the king of Canaan.

In times of war the Lord often raises up prophets. Whenever there is great conflict, God will raise up men and women to hear His voice from heaven and bring it down for that time and season. I feel that today the Lord is telling us that we are living in a time for not only the Esthers (the younger generation) and the Annas and Simeons (the older generation), but also the Deborahs, the mothers of Israel, to come up into place. Against great odds, Deborah stood as a powerful intercessor and deliverer of her people.

I believe that God is releasing special anointing on women because they have been missing in action. Many women have gone AWOL—or else are imprisoned within cultural and religious systems. The Lord wants to set women free. He wants to raise up a company of end time Deborahs. He is calling women to be part of the army of the Lord, to learn to move strategically as His government invades the earth.

This wonderful story also champions men and women partnering together at the battle stations. When Deborah gave a word of the Lord to the military commander, Barak, telling him to arise and follow certain instructions to engage the Canaanites in battle, he responded with godly fear. He recognized that she was a prophet of God, that she had the word of the Lord for the hour.

So his response was, "If you will go with me, then I will go" (Judges 4:8).

Deborah replied,

118

I will surely go with you; nevertheless there will be no glory for you in the journey you are taking, for the LORD will sell Sisera into the hand of a woman [who was the housewife Jael].

Judges 4:9

Deborah heard the voice of the Lord regarding strategizing a military invasion, and she knew how to be a standard-bearer and legislator. She was able to stand with Barak, both of them moving governmentally.

Our times and seasons are not very different. One minute we might be sitting under a palm tree, that symbol of righteousness, hearing strategies for different people around us. The next minute we might be going into battle.

This gives us another insight: We could lose our lives in this war! You see, when Deborah went to war, she knew it was a suicide mission. Barak's army of ten thousand Israelites was challenging an army that was ten times bigger and equipped with nine hundred iron chariots. They needed a miracle.

What happened? An amazing string of events.

First God gave Deborah revelation of how to win the battle and then a prophetic word when it was time to rout the enemy (see Judges 4:6–7, 14).

In a moment of crisis she decreed the word of the Lord, and creation bowed to her command: The heavens broke open with such creative anointing that even the stars moved on the army's behalf (see Judges 5:20).

Seeing in the heavens and moving with prophetic proclamations, she released warrior angels of the Lord to fight ancient demonic principalities (see Judges 5:23).

And finally a providential storm (see Judges 5:4) flooded the plain, making the much-feared chariots useless. The enemy was slaughtered by the Israelites and washed away by a flash flood (see Judges 5:21).

Deborah's actions brought holy reversal to the enemy's evil plans. Her prayers and military leadership shifted the course of history and saved the nation of Israel.

Today, as the thundering chariots and galloping horses race down the battlefield toward us, all we can do is say, "I know that I heard God. I stand on that. I stand on the prophetic word." We need a miracle, too, and we can be sure that God is releasing prophetic words like fire from heaven to melt mountains and flood rivers. As He gives prophetic proclamations, even the stars in the heavens will fight against the demonic powers and principalities. There will be blood, but there will also be salvation, deliverance and healing.

Deborah shows us how to listen for the word of the Lord and go into battle with courage. Her choice could have been costly, and ours could be, too, but we are warriors who know how to dream and who know how to love. I think that we will be amazed at the ways in which God moves on our behalf.

Joshua: Following Divine Strategies

This brings us to Joshua. His journey took place 175 years before Deborah's inspiring story. He led the original conquest that dispossessed the Canaanites and claimed the Promised Land.

His battle, too, shows that God will give supernatural power to fulfill prophetic words spoken by His warriors. In a time when Joshua had no hope apart from the Lord, the strategies he received were truly unusual and creative. The Lord required prophetic acts that seem utterly ridiculous to the natural mind. Hide in a brothel? Scandalous! Believe that city walls will simply fall down if you march around them seven times while blowing a horn? Preposterous!

In this critical season, our global, local and personal situations also look impossible. When our circumstances overwhelm us and when giants roam freely across the land, the Lord promises us that He is faithful. Our job is to be obedient and trust.

How do we start to move in warfare like Joshua, developing strategies and partnering with the Holy Spirit? Sometimes when we come up against a fortified city, we start by asking the Lord what the strongholds are. If He reveals the belief systems at work, He will lead the battle to take them down.

Mission Impossible

Joshua's story involves two spy missions. It takes us back for a moment to the leadership of Moses. We have seen how he was a great deliverer of his people. He was a close friend of almighty God. He had astonishing visitations and actually glowed physically with the presence of the Lord. He also brought the children of Israel to the border of the Promised Land. Now it was time for the people to take their inheritance.

Following God's directions, Moses sent twelve men to spy out the land of Canaan. This spy team stayed on assignment for forty days. When it returned, the results were not what the people expected. Ten of the spies gave a bad report. They saw in the land men of great stature and felt like grasshoppers compared to them. Only Joshua and Caleb argued for following the Lord and taking the land. "Wait a minute!" they shouted. "We have a God who can help us take that land. He has promised it to us. Yes, there are giants and fortified cities, but we have a God who can break in with an invasion of heaven and help us."

But the hearts of the people shriveled with fear. They would have none of it. They wept and said that Moses should have left them in Egypt. They wanted to stone

Moses and Aaron and elect a new leader. This did not make God happy. It is not a good idea to stone your leaders! It is also not a good idea to rebel against the word of the Lord. For their faithlessness and disobedience, God said that they would wander in the wilderness for forty years. A whole generation—with the exception of Joshua and Caleb—would have to die.

Then even Moses broke faith, striking a rock in a way that misrepresented God to the people. He was 120 years old, his eyes were clear and he was strong. He could see the Promised Land from a distance, but he could not go in.

This should cause us to consider our own vision. When we talk about taking territory for the Lord, what is our perspective? Do we see only the giants and the fortified cities? Do we see only land that will devour its inhabitants? Do we see ourselves with the mind-set that "We are just grasshoppers"? Do we act rashly and miss the opportunity to fulfill our destinies?

As a result of their perspective, a whole generation suffered. I feel that the Body of Christ is standing poised at a prophetic dividing line. We are coming into a season in which we will be either a Moses generation or a Joshua generation. With Moses, the people could look back and say, "Yes, we had miracles. The Lord gave us manna every day. He provided for us." They had history.

But they also had a slave mentality. None of the miracles ever really satisfied them. The acts of God did not draw their hearts to Him.

We can fall into that same trap. We want what the Holy Spirit has to offer—we recall here Rebekah's gold bracelet, fine clothes, lavish gifts—but we need to remember that there is a deeper motivation than gifts alone: The Holy Spirit is drawing us to the Bridegroom King. He is looking for a Bride, not a slave.

The Lord wants to move us as a church without walls so that we can reach hurt and dying people. He wants

122

us to start to fulfill our destinies as warriors who love to dream. We know that there are giants in the land, but are we willing to partner with the Holy Spirit so He can give us creative strategies and war plans?

New Leadership

This was the challenge Joshua faced when he came into leadership at the death of Moses.

How was Joshua prepared by the Lord for this moment? Joshua had served as Moses' personal servant and he, too, had hunger for the glory of the Lord. When Moses entered the Tabernacle to meet with God, Scripture says that "he would return to the camp, but his servant Joshua the son of Nun, a young man, did not depart from the tabernacle" (Exodus 33:11). He was hungry; he would stay around the tent to linger in the presence. Numbers 27:18 refers to Joshua as one in whom the Spirit dwelt. He understood prophetic vision.

Finally after forty long years of wandering, it was time to take the land. Joshua wanted to get war strategies. He wanted to know how to take the city. So two spies slipped across the Jordan into Jericho in the land of Canaan.

Now, great fear had come on the city of Jericho because the people knew all about the God of the Israelites who had parted the Red Sea. They knew, perhaps instinctively, that God was going to destroy the city of Jericho. They may have been aware, as well, that the Canaanites had the curse of Noah on them. Every man, woman and child in Jericho was going to die. They understood this and had great fear.

One person saw an opportunity to save herself and her household, and she leapt at the chance. This was a woman named Rahab, a prostitute. She realized the men were spies for Israel and gave them shelter. In return, she asked that she and her family be spared.

I am sure the two spies were astonished to find faith like hers in the house of a prostitute. They agreed to her proposal—promising to "deal kindly and truly" (Joshua 2:14) with her. When the time came for them to slip out of the city, Rahab helped them escape out a window by lowering them down the city wall on a scarlet cord.

Where did she get a scarlet cord? Her robes were most likely made of scarlet. She probably tore the robes to make a rope that would lower the spies to safety. She also told them to hide in the hills for three days before making their way back to their camp, a strategy that further ensured their safety. They were able to report that the Lord was indeed delivering this land into their hands.

We will talk more about Rahab in a moment.

Holy Covenant, Holy War

Now this was during flood season and was not normally the time to try to cross the Jordan. But the Lord said, "Now is the time. I want you to go through the Jordan." Many times we look at our circumstances and say, "Lord, this is impossible. How can we get through the Jordan? How can we do this? What should we do?"

Joshua did not question the Lord's directive, though, and he began to receive divine strategies on how to move. The Lord told Joshua to have the priests carry the Ark, the presence of the Lord. He said that as they moved forward the waters would recede.

It happened just as the Lord had said. Joshua and the children of Israel crossed the river into the Promised Land, and all the fortified cities were even more terrified because of it. Joshua 5:1 says that their hearts melted and they no longer had the courage to face the Israelites. This seemed like the optimal time to rush into battle.

But the Lord again chose an unusual strategy. These warriors were prepared to fight, yet the Lord made them vulnerable: He wanted the males who had been born in the wilderness to be circumcised. Circumcision identified a male as a child of Abraham and qualified him for the covenant blessings. This was a holy covenant for holy war.

God was teaching them the importance of relationship; He wanted to enter into covenant with them. He was asking them to sacrifice their physical strength on an altar of devotion and loyalty. They were now in a position of weakness. They could not capture Jericho in their own strength; they could barely walk. They chose, by taking part in this covenant, to trust God to protect and guide them.

Holy Visitation

The Lord responded to their faith by meeting with Joshua in an amazing visitation and giving him directions for their victory over Jericho: "A Man stood opposite him with His sword drawn in His hand" (Joshua 5:13). The directions He gave are familiar to us now—march around the city with the Ark of the Covenant daily for six days, then march while blowing rams' horns and shouting on the seventh day.

What an incredible story! What a unique strategy! No commander on earth would plan for battle like that. Who would go to war when your front line of protection is a group of trumpet-playing priests? But we know the happy ending: Joshua fought the battle of Jericho, and the walls came tumbling down.

So what are the giants we face today? What are the strongholds that rob us of faith and enslave us to fear? As we believe God and take even baby steps of faith, He will give us creative strategies for winning the battles.

We have seen so far that our times and seasons depend on hearing the word like Deborah and expecting unexpected strategies like Joshua. And this brings us to Rahab, a symbol of the great harvest before us.

125

Rahab: Touching Society

Rahab was a harlot in a doomed city. The spies were on a godly mission to fulfill the destiny of their people. You might not think that these individuals had much in common, but in the strategy of God they did: They all saw an open door and walked through it.

The spies saw a door that was open for trade in the house of a prostitute. They considered it a good place to hide. If you go into the house of a prostitute, normally people will not be asking you for your ID.

And Rahab? She saw an open door to her salvation. By helping the spies, and later joining their numbers, she saved her life and the lives of her family members.

This story helps us rethink our strategies for evangelism. The people whom we might think are enemies of God, and therefore not associate with, are the very ones whom the Lord might use us to reach.

So what does Rahab look like today? Maybe she wears designer clothes. She goes to the mall. She sleeps with whatever man she is dating. She might be addicted to prescription drugs. There are a thousand different faces and a thousand different stories we could paint. The unifying point would be that we live in a world where it is not uncommon to make many choices that grieve God and hinder our destinies from being fulfilled. Thus, as He starts to take His soldiers into Jericho, He asks if we are willing to look for the open doors that He can take us through strategically. Rahab was an enemy to the Law of Moses, but when she saw her chance for redemption, she did not let the opportunity pass.

Rahab, in the Word of God, is called "righteous" (James 2:25, NIV) because her actions saved the lives of the spies and helped ensure the Israelites' victory in battle. She later married an Israelite named Salmon and was the mother of Boaz, who was the great-grandfather of King David (see

Matthew 1:5–6). She was actually an ancestor of Jesus (see Matthew 1:1–16; Luke 3:23–38)! The writer of Hebrews applauds her example of faith (see Hebrews 11:31). James notes that her works were the practical expression of her faith (see James 2:25). What if the spies had never knocked on her door?

Because of her response to a move of God in her midst, she is part of the Body, the Bride of Christ. This prostitute, whose door was open for business, now dances with the King in garments of white. His love will transform a prostitute into a heroine, a harlot into a pure and spotless bride! God does not look at fallen humanity as we do. He has the ravished heart of a Bridegroom.

There are so many broken ones whom the Lord wants to heal and save. He wants us to take off our blinders. He wants us to see those people in our neighborhoods who do not quite measure up to what we would expect to find in church. We need to hear His cry for us to move in bridal partnership. We can be ones who move throughout the harvest to gather the people God has called to be part of the Body.

This is a love message. Rahab is a prophetic picture of the end time Church. The Bride of Christ will be birthed from the most unlikely places. He comes and finds these devastated, hurting, despised, culturally rejected and broken people and tells them He loves them. He says, "I will fill your empty heart. I will clothe you. I will take away your rags. You will no longer be called forsaken and desolate. I call you Beulah. I call you married one."

Do we tend to go only on mission trips to the "poor"? Or do we hear the Lord when we are in board meetings, in coffee shops, in schools or in the computer world? Do we say, "Lord, start to give me divine strategies. I want to hear Your word. I am willing to go into battle. Show me Your plans for the end time harvest"?

127

As we go into our places of work or schools or ministries, we need to see them as a "Jericho" and ask the Lord to show us the doors of the people who are ready for a divine appointment. This is not business as usual. This is a season of war. It is also a season of divine partnership, clarity, discernment and pressing into prayer. We need to be asking for strategies to touch the Rahabs in our world.

In other words, while the battlefield is in the heavenlies, we gather the harvest right here on earth. We will talk about heavenly encounters in the next chapter, and we will explore specific strategies for soldiers in the chapter following that, so I want to focus for the rest of this chapter on the wonderful experience of bringing in the lost—especially those who might seem like the most unlikely candidates.

An Unchurched Church

Several years ago I visited a large church in Copenhagen, Denmark, because I had heard that a Nigerian healing evangelist was having meetings there. He was the talk of the town. In Denmark only one percent of the people is saved, yet large crowds were staying past midnight because the Lord was healing the sick.

It was ten at night when I first heard about this; I had been ministering in another city. I was interested to go to the church, so my host couple took me. When we arrived, we saw probably fifteen hundred people there. And they loved it! You could see and feel their enthusiasm.

When I looked at the crowd, I could tell they were mostly an unchurched group. Along with many businessmen and women, there were people in the occult, Yuppies, prostitutes, artists, street people—people from every walk of life imaginable. Broken, hurting people were getting prayer for everything from cancer to all kinds of deformities. The people were standing or sitting, waiting for hours to get prayer for healing. Miracles were happening everywhere. The people were intrigued!

I met the pastor and said, "I love the people! I can tell that they are not a church crowd. How did you get them here?"

He said, "Well, Jill, we just advertise. We advertise in all of the New Age papers and in all of the secular papers. We say, 'Are you sick? Are you in pain? Do you need a miracle?' Many people come who don't know the Lord. They get healed and they end up accepting Him. We have more than eight hundred people who have just signed up for the Alpha [Bible teaching] course from our week of meetings. We will start to disciple them, but they came because they got a miracle and the power of the Gospel was demonstrated."

He went on to say, "A lot of people get hurt in churches, and they leave for 'seeker-friendly' places that have more of a 'social' gospel or an 'intellectual' gospel. They don't want to get hurt again. And they don't want the emotionalism that can come with the Spirit-filled churches. So they find churches that may have great biblical teaching but no demonstration of the power of God. There is the Word, but there is not much of the Spirit. They will go for their forty-five minutes, and then they want to get their kids home.

"But those in the world are not jaded by the power of God. They have not been in controversial moves of the Holy Spirit. They want a display of signs and wonders. So often we feel that if God starts to grip people, we will offend the unsaved. The reality is that we offend the Church, the religious folks, the Pharisees. We offend the people who have a controlling spirit."

That experience reminded me of Paul's missionary trip through Asia Minor (see Acts 19:1–10). Ephesus was a stronghold of witchcraft. The people he preached to had been exposed to sorcery; they were open in their spirits to the demonic realm. So when they saw the signs and wonders that the Lord worked through Paul and his team, they recognized *true* power. It was easy to bring them to the cross with Jesus.

The government of God backed up Paul's words with such extraordinary signs and wonders that an entire continent was touched in two years! As Paul explained,

> My speech and my preaching were not with persuasive words of human wisdom, but in demonstration of the Spirit and of power, that your faith should not be in the wisdom of men but in the power of God.
>
> 1 Corinthians 2:4–5

Beloved, it will take more than just eloquent teaching to touch this generation. *We must have the power of God!* We need to cry out for a fresh baptism of fire—another Pentecost—if we want this magnitude of revival in our cities.

Can you imagine the Gospel spreading so quickly that even the pagan leaders of other countries would be saved? If it happened two thousand years ago, why not today, too? When there is a demonstration of the Holy Spirit's power, entire nations will be transformed.

Going Fishing

You can be part of this. You are a member of a handpicked brigade of fishermen. Jesus has been mending the holes in your nets so that you can cast them into the dark seas of humanity. The Shekinah glory will spread as it hits the water, and the fish will be drawn to it. When He is lifted up, all men draw near. Now is the hour!

Can you feel God's heartbeat? Can you hear what He hears? Can you feel what He feels? If you know the heart of God, then you can also awaken your heart for the people around you. That is how you move in the prophetic and give words of encouragement and draw people into the Kingdom, because you catch the dream, the dream of God. You catch a glimpse of the destiny for the person next to you. Then when you give a word, it is a word of life. When the person next to you is drowning in a sea of lost dreams, you can throw out the lifeline—the words of hope—and pull him out.

This is like going fishing—deep-sea fishing. It is safer and easier to go after the little fish near the shore; it is much more challenging to evangelize in the deep waters. But people are dying out in the great seas of humanity. Sometimes all the fishing boats need to connect their nets because the catch is so great.

Do you see why evangelism does not work according to a religious system? People do not want to be caught up in a system; plus, they may know how the system works and not be interested. But if you are watching and praying and listening to God's heart, you know if a divine strategy is unfolding.

In these times and seasons, it is about being authentic and real in everyday life. Where do you walk? Where do you take your shoes off? That is your territory. Are you someone like me—in many cities and airports and always on the go? Or is your territory your house with pool parties or barbecues for neighbors? Not everyone is called to a Third World country. Do you recognize your mission field? Whom are you touching? Who is crossing your path?

When I was ministering in Berlin, Germany, the Lord pointed out to me a young man who was sitting way in the back of the church, and He told me to bring him to the front for a prophetic word. As the young man moved down the aisle, I could hear gasps from those he passed. This muscle-bound young man had a Mohawk and tattoos, and he was dressed in leather and chains.

I had to have an interpreter, naturally, but as I gave prophetic words and he received the interpretation, his head would quickly turn to look at me. His puzzled expressions were saying, *How did you know that?* The words were causing him to cup his hands over his mouth and giggle like a little boy, which was so contrary to his appearance.

Then the Lord told me to call forward a couple who were in that same row because they were somehow connected to this young man. I did not know until later that they had been witnessing to him and had brought him to the service.

More words flowed, and the couple nodded in agreement when I said, "And the Lord has told me that He is going to heal the wounding between you and your father." This young man burst into tears. He met Jesus that night and the crowd cheered.

As these three returned to their seats, the Lord told me to challenge the people regarding marketplace evangelism. "If you saw this young man around town," I said, "would you talk to him and share Jesus with him?" They shook their heads. At least they were honest! But the Lord wanted to make a point. "And why not?" I asked. "Because of his appearance?" This time they nodded.

I told them that I had grown up in the church, gotten into the hippie movement and I returned as a prodigal. After one particular service, I was out on the steps having a cigarette, debating with God that these church people were too straight and conservative and religious for me; maybe I would never make it there. Most of the people who walked by me gave me judgmental looks because of my smoking and my clay-covered overalls. (I had been up all night in the pottery studio, firing kilns.)

But Karen, a young artist with a gift of prophetic evangelism, approached me and invited me to lunch at the home of her friend Patti, a widow who had seven children. Patti became a spiritual mom to both of us, and we would often hang out at her home. Karen has been one of my dearest and closest friends for several decades now. She included me in her life instead of judging me. What if she had not approached me because of *my* appearance?

Jesus demonstrated prophetic evangelism. He did only what He saw His Father do. Wherever He went, that is where His mission field was. And we have to understand that in our day, in our time, wherever we are in this moment, whatever our next step, whoever the next person—that is our mission field. Yes, we have long-term goals. But we are also saying that we accept our journeys, our destinies, right now.

Whenever there is great conflict, God raises up men and women to hear His voice from heaven and speak His word for that time and that season. As we move into great shakings on the earth today, the Lord is going to raise up many of us to stand in His counsels, to bring down wisdom and revelation, to legislate those decrees and to usher in a great harvest of souls.

This is the first time in the history of the world that the majority of Christians believes we are living in the generation when Jesus will return. This is not a time for church as usual. The Lord is mobilizing global prayer warriors to invade the kingdom of darkness and set many captives free.

When we move in these realms, two things happen. One, the warriors go into the heavens, see what is happening and have an impact on their world. Two, the battle gets hotter as the enemy responds with assaults. We will look at an example of this in the next chapter.

8

Encounters
on the Battlefield

Is the power and presence of God evident in your life? Are you moving in His power to help save the lost? Then you are probably finding that warfare is increasing around you. Just when you get a couple of feet ahead, the enemy comes. With higher anointing come higher devils. You get promoted so you get both. You think you are going to get a lot of God and a little attack, but you normally get a lot of God and a lot of attack. This is true even if you do not like being a fighter. Basically you can either be a fighter or be plowed under. Civilians are usually the first casualties in a war.

That is why the Body of Christ has to mature. We have to know how to pray for ourselves and others who are out on the battlefield.

The Battle Heats Up

I would like to tell you a war story that illustrates this. I mentioned earlier that years ago my ministry produced many dramas in which my character portrayed the Master Potter, the father heart of God. One particular drama, "The Empty Cradle," dealt with abortion issues. Abortion was not talked about in the church or anywhere else in the 1980s, so our drama was "outside the box" in the church culture. But God directed me to put together a presentation that would address this "holocaust in the womb," as He called it.

As I created a beautiful clay vessel, which represented a child in the womb, a huge multimedia presentation showed the journey of his life—from the womb, through his childhood, getting married, having his own children and pursuing a breakthrough medical career. As part of the drama, the young couple decided to have an abortion and the "child's" life was ended on the potter's wheel.

The drama served as an interactive experience for women who had had abortions and for men who had forced their girlfriends and wives to have abortions. Both were able to experience forgiveness from Father God. We had prayer teams and counselors praying for people throughout the evening.

We were shocked at the strong grieving reactions from those watching the drama. Many began sobbing as the Lord lifted the veil from their eyes and minds to see what abortion was really all about—the genocide of generations. Most people in our audiences had no idea of the physical and emotional consequences of abortion, but we encountered them consistently when ministering to the women: guilt, shame, health problems, sleepless nights hearing their babies crying, depression and thoughts of suicide.

God directed everything about the play. He gave me specific visions and words as I prepared the drama. It was birthed in my spirit before I put it on paper. When I finally sat down and wrote it, it just flowed and took only a few weeks. But when we started to put the drama together—lining up actors, actresses, music—we were hit by a demonic backlash that was unprecedented since the beginning of the ministry.

The last three or four times we presented the drama, for instance, the actresses literally threw up blood before the performances. Mary, one of my closest team members, was in charge of orchestrating the multimedia presentation. She ended up in the hospital twice with bronchial pneumonia, which almost took her life. Another team member had a serious car accident. Some of the team members could not handle the warfare and left.

We were not performing a play for the entertainment of the church; we were exposing and confronting a spirit of death, and there were casualties. Satan hated the freedom that people were finding and wanted the drama stopped!

At one point we were ministering in a large church in California. Everything was working great the first hour of the service, but as soon as they handed me the microphone, the theatrical lights and sound stopped working. When the equipment was finally back in operation, the multimedia part of our drama jammed. We encountered incredible warfare that night; abortion is a powerful stronghold of the enemy.

Usually at the conclusion of the drama we invited anyone to come forward for prayer who was experiencing deep repentance over abortions. This time, however, the Lord gave me further instructions. He said, *Jill, I don't want you to call up just those who have had abortions. You need to confront people who are buying into the spirit of death. They are asking Me to take them home—they want to die—because they hurt so badly. Tell them that is Christian suicide. They have become numb and have shut their hearts down because their dreams and destinies also seem as though they have been aborted.*

I understood Him to be telling me that not only did the people want to save their unborn children from the pain of life, but they wanted their lives to be over, as well. So we gave the invitation to all of those who had told the Lord to take them home because they did not want to live. Almost the entire audience came forward. They went through repentance, deliverance and great restoration. Satan lost a lot of ground that night.

The assaults from the enemy seemed only to increase after this. Soon I began to feel an odd sensation. It was as if I had a stake in my spirit, a fiery dart of the enemy. I did not understand what that meant exactly; I just knew I had been wounded. I felt as though I was "bleeding" and my mantle was torn.

I spent months praying about this. I knew that it was an Antichrist spirit, a spirit of death, but I did not know how to break it. Finally I said, "Lord, I need someone to pray for me. I am hurting. I need someone to break off some of the attack from the enemy." At that time I did not know any intercessors who understood spiritual warfare at that level—including myself. Several people prayed faithfully for me, but they did not yet have the anointing and authority in the Spirit to take on that kind of warfare.

I asked the Lord to take His searchlight and reveal any areas of sin in my life and scrub my heart clean. If I had any open doors where the enemy could have legal access to my life, I wanted to repent and close them.

Soon after that, the Lord set up a divine appointment for me to meet Cindy Jacobs, who became a lifelong friend that day. (Cindy is cofounder of Generals International.) We had lunch and I mentioned, "Have you ever prayed for anyone who has a stake in her?"

"Yes," she said. "It's witchcraft coming against you. I'll pray for you." We went back to my house, and she was able to break the power of the enemy and pull out the fiery dart after about twenty minutes of prayer. I learned a great deal about warfare that day. But the battle was not over.

A Heavenly Visitation

Soon after she left, I spent time before the Lord, thanking Him.

That night, the power of the Lord came upon me. It was as though liquid fire came over my body, causing me to shake with the power of God. Then, every day at about three in the afternoon, the Lord would meet me and His presence would stay with me until seven the next morning. This happened for 21 days.

I know now that visitations can happen in public places, but often the more intense and prolonged encounters happen in your home or in a place where God can meet you privately. The power of God comes on you and He shows you your heart. It is a very intimate thing. Sometimes you will be on the floor, travailing for hours.

All I knew at the time was that God had given me a revelation of Himself such as I had never experienced in my whole life. He showed me things in my heart that needed to come out. He revealed areas where I thought I had repented, but where there was deeper work to be done.

Then He showed me different kinds of fire and started to give me revelation as to the fires' relevance to praying for others. I can remember weeping and weeping as the fire of the Lord was on me, revealing His heart for the lost. There are some things that I cannot even share because they take me places beyond words.

I knew I was experiencing a visitation, and I knew it was a promotion in the Spirit, although I did not understand what that meant at the time. We see in a mirror dimly. But I share this experience with you because I want to explain two things about warfare: One, there is always a price. Whenever God meets with you and gives you revelation into mysteries, the enemy will come at you with an assault. Two, we need to be strong in the Lord so we can move in discernment. Otherwise our prayers will not be effective.

Since this visitation, in all of the different meetings and churches I go to, I notice that things are different: The anointing is higher and stronger. I move with more of a corporate anointing as the heavens open and the atmosphere of God comes into the meetings. When I pray for people, I know things about their future and know things that have happened to them in the past by the revelation of the Spirit. Often when I lay my hands on people I can feel "spears" or bondage or see afflicting spirits. I receive words of knowledge faster. People are set free more quickly. It is as if there is an intense revelation of His heart moving throughout the room.

When you have an encounter in heaven, you bring a touch of heaven to earth. It is a growing process. He is still teaching me how to use my hands, which were in His fire during the visitation. He is showing me how to use my eyes, which were with Him in the heavens, and my ears, which became more fine-tuned. I can hear His whispers and His nudges. He will say, *Jill, do this,* or, *Do that.* It is very exciting!

When you have a powerful encounter with the Lord, remember always to guard your heart from pride. Be watchful. When you get a promotion in the Spirit, there will be stronger demonic attacks coming against you. The warfare grows stronger. So while you are with the Lord, asking Him to teach you how to fight, how to use your armor, how to follow Him with discernment and keenness in your spirit, the enemy is gathering his ranks around you to take you down. Remember Moses: Before he even got down the mountain, the enemy was lining up assaults.

Another Battle

Six months after this visitation, our ministry team had a meeting in the inner city of Los Angeles. The meeting was wonderful, and the Lord came with great power. But I knew at the end of the meeting that, once again, I had been cursed.

The next day I could barely get out of bed. Over the next several days I woke up with terrible migraine headaches. I wound up in the emergency room. I learned that I had sinusitis. I went home and several days later I was back at the hospital because of the intense pain. This time they told me I also had some other "itis." The pain did not stop.

After a return trip to the hospital ten or twelve days later, I learned I had shingles, which affects the nerve endings. One side of my face up to my scalp had broken out in huge blisters. I could not wear my contacts because my face and eye were so swollen.

I lay in bed on my back for fourteen days. I was in too much pain even to listen to music. The doctor told me that if the shingles continued to spread on my face to the tip of my nose, I would go blind in my right eye. He said if it continued past my nose, I could die. They could not give me any medication.

I called several of my praying friends, and they told me that they were seeing visions of people in circles praying against me, curses coming against me with an evil eye and more. They were able to reveal many pieces of the puzzle, but once again I was stuck with affliction and no remedy.

I was close to dying, yet I could not get the help I needed. I had had a visitation of glorious things for 21 days. Now I had been in bed afflicted for 21 days.

Then, miraculously, Cindy, who had prayed previously and pulled the stake out of me, was holding a meeting near my home. A friend took me to the meeting, but I could not stay in the room because I was in too much pain. I managed to get to the ladies' room.

Cindy saw me leave and followed me. She prayed with me in the bathroom for five or ten minutes. I could feel the sickness literally breaking off of my head. Within the next two hours, my eye opened. It was a miracle!

You see, if we are going to be successful on the battlefield, we must train our hands to be weapons of war. We must be on our faces with visitations and the power of the Holy Spirit falling on us to be able to pray with anointing and authority. Nothing less is going to set the captives free.

Counting the Cost

Now you may be asking yourself why you would want to stay in such a war when the soldiers can be so beaten and bloodied. If you are a follower of Christ, you have no choice. You are in His army. You are already at war. If you think that the enemy will leave you alone as long as you keep quiet, then you must rethink your commitment to your Captain and your fellow soldiers. Jesus tells us to take up our crosses and follow Him. Will we refuse? Those around us in the battle are going to be wounded. Are we going to turn our faces from their need?

And besides, there is a price behind the anointing, but there is an even greater price when you do nothing and let the enemy ravage you and your loved ones. He has no mercy.

We are like the Roman soldiers in ancient times who lined up arm in arm and walked with their shields in front of them. They became a human wall. They stood as one, and that made the army strong.

Or think about boot camp today. Young men and women sign up for the military and usually find it to be the most physically and mentally challenging experience they will ever have. Basic training is intentionally difficult because it is designed to flush weakness from the body and soul. Any recruits who come with preconceived ideas of their limitations will find that the military spends a lot of time shattering those notions. Their weakness turns to strength, and the transformation is stunning.

Soldiers are trained to rely on one another because that is what may make or break a mission out in the field. It is not a game. It could cost their lives and, ultimately, the freedom of their nation.

Well, it is not so different for us as Christian warriors. Spiritual warfare has many things in common with natural warfare. If we are self-focused and self-protective, we are opening the Body to wounding or defeat. We need a unified Body. We need our arms locked. Some may be commissioned to strategize, some to lead small groups, some to pray for the sick. Our callings may vary, but we need to be able to operate as one. We need to connect on these deeper levels, locking our hearts like shields.

Now let's discover specific strategies that help us on the battlefield.

9

Strategies for Soldiers

As the Lord takes us through boot camp and intensive training, we can ask ourselves a number of questions that help us gauge how well we are growing in our understanding of how to move in the anointing: Can I hear the voice of God for myself? Am I asking Him to open my ears so I can hear Him? Do I trust the nudges that He gives me? If I get part of a picture, do I ask Him for more? Or do I always feel that I am making it up? Have I asked the Lord to give me dreams in the night? Have I told Him I am on call any time of the day or night? Have I asked Him to wake me in the middle of the night to hear His voice and learn from Him?

We learn by doing. I certainly did not wake up one morning, hear God's voice clearly and step into a ministry that carries me all over the world. Far from it. When I came to the Lord, I was so shy and fearful I was incapable of hugging the person next to me in church. Jesus has done tremendous work in my life about that.

No one wants to make mistakes and hurt people. If, however, we have to have everything lined up perfectly before we step forward in ministry, we will most likely miss the move of the Holy Spirit. We must be willing to go forward in the midst of not knowing how.

God wants His soldiers to be carriers of resurrection life. He wants us to move in ways that help people be saved, healed and delivered. Who did that best? Jesus, of course. God sent Jesus to reach people in ways that they could relate to. To the fishermen He talked fish. To the field people He talked crops. To the tax collectors He talked money. To a woman with a pitcher He sat by a well and talked water. He was able to walk alongside anyone and speak his or her language. God is relational, and He trains His soldiers to be like Him.

Training Skills

There are many important strategies every soldier of the Lord needs to know, which I will cover in a moment. First I want to mention two well-known but often overlooked principles that are foundational.

One is the great commandment to love Jesus with all of your heart; the other is to love your neighbor as yourself. To walk this out practically, He wants you to be a living witness—to use your mouth to speak His words; to stretch forth your hands in signs and wonders; to use your feet to be a carrier of the Good News.

God wants us to learn to hear His voice and operate in the prophetic. The purpose is not so that we can be fortune-tellers but so that we can bring the lost into the Kingdom. Just as Jesus ministered to each person in a unique way, so God wants us to learn to hear His voice for each individual and deliver the Gospel in a tailor-made package. This might mean buying one person a cup of coffee. It might mean giving someone else a word of knowledge or prophecy. Or God might want you to heal someone in the grocery store.

Whatever He says to do, we can enjoy the adventure. God is full of surprises! He will help us move in His power in order to bring the unsaved into the Body. In other words, revival and war are running mates; training for one enhances the other. Here, then, are a number of strategies.

Start Small

Sometimes we get a word from the Lord that we know He wants us to share, but there is a problem: We have only part of the message. Let me assure you that this is normal! As we step out in obedience and speak what we have heard, Jesus gives the next part. We cannot wait for a vision in Technicolor to be projected on the wall before we start to obey. We begin with small impressions. More will follow.

An ideal place to learn how to receive and give words from the Lord is in home or cell groups. I remember driving to a home group many years ago and telling the Lord, "Here I am. I'm available." I really wanted to hear from Him.

During worship I heard from Him, but it was not what I expected. In my mind's eye I saw a flower.

I knew that He wanted me to tell the group what I was seeing. My heart started beating faster.

I argued with Him. *God, it's just a flower!* Then about that time one of the men in the group gave a prophetic word that started, "Thus saith the Lord. . . ." I told the Lord I did not know how to speak King James' English. Then I noticed that some of the petals on the flower were plucked off.

My inner argument continued. *Lord,* I said, *it's a flower with petals plucked off. What am I supposed to say: "Thus saith the Lord, 'I see a flower'"?*

Finally, with much fear, I began: "I see a flower." And then somehow I had more understanding of His message. I continued: "And even though some of the petals are plucked off, God still loves you." People actually wept. It was so simple.

The next week I again told the Lord that I was available. In the middle of the meeting, during the worship time, the Lord gave me another picture. This time He showed me a fish.

God, I groaned inwardly, *not again. It's a fish.* As I looked at the fish I saw that it was talking. I knew they would think I was crazy. But once again, with my heart ready to pound out of my chest, I said, "I see this fish. I see it in a fishbowl saying, 'Let me out of the bowl. Let me out of the bowl.'" After I said that, I saw the next part of the word, which was a shark coming to devour it. The Lord told me that if He let the fish out of the bowl too soon, the shark would eat it. I learned that this applied to a situation that someone had been praying about.

I had been attending that group for about three months when the Lord gave me another word. There were about seventy people in the home that evening, all sitting on the floor, worshiping. All of a sudden, I saw a mental picture of the house we were meeting in. I thought, *Well, this is good; it's not a fish!* I felt pleased at what promised to be evidence of my growing ability to hear.

Then I saw a dark thundercloud come over the house. I thought, *Uh, oh.* I watched as the hand of the Lord came out of the cloud with a sword and cut the house in half. He gave me these words: *No longer will there be meetings here.* This was the home of four Christian women and God revealed to me their gossip, slander and so forth.

Now at this point, I was sweating bullets. I said, *God, I don't want that word! Give that word to one of the men. They would like to give a heavy word like that. I want the simple word. Where is the fish?*

He said, *Give the word.*

I was terrified. I kept telling the Lord about my fears, and He kept giving me more information.

The singing and praises drifted to a stop. I closed my eyes, took a deep breath and with tremendous hesitation I finally gave the word. When I opened my eyes, everyone else's eyes were open, too, as well as their mouths.

I thought they might say, "Congratulations, sister, that took courage." I was so young in the Lord I did not know that I was shutting down the meeting.

Finally the leader said, "I think there are snacks in the kitchen." Literally the whole group of seventy people stood and stampeded out of the room, leaving me sitting there all by myself.

I grabbed my purse, ran to my car and wept as I drove home. I prayed, *Lord, I thought I saw it. I guess I missed it.* For the next three days, all I could do was cry. But then the home group leader called me and said, "Jill, your word was right on. We have moved our meeting to another house."

I made a covenant with the Lord that day that my journey would always include being available to Him. There were other times that I did not know how to talk to, much less pray for, people, but I could start small. I promised that I would always be available and would let Him teach me.

Honestly, it does not take much to see different kinds of sin or brokenness on people. The world does not try to hide these things. The Lord will meet you in situations where He will give you a living word and that word will pierce the darkness and bring the lost into the Kingdom.

Always Rest

Do you know that rest is a form of spiritual warfare? "In quietness and confidence shall be your strength" (Isaiah 30:15); "Come to Me, all you who labor and are heavy laden, and I will give you rest" (Matthew 11:28); "Because You have been my help, therefore in the shadow of Your wings I will rejoice. My soul follows close behind You; Your right hand upholds me" (Psalm 63:7–8).

We go to war out of rest. Rest is first. The Sabbath is the first day of the week, not the last day of the week. It is not work and be tired and then rest. It is rest, get our batteries charged and then go. We tend to have an abundance of ideas and rush into our programs and not wait on the Holy Spirit. We fail to rest, and then we break down and are forced to rest. There is a lot of exhaustion that is not from God.

Rest also helps us when Satan attacks. Scripture tells us that the enemy "shall speak words against the Most High [God] and shall wear out the saints of the Most High" (Daniel 7:25, AMPLIFIED). He wants to wear out and destroy the soldiers of the Lord. We must remember that his work among us is not always apparent; it goes on silently day after week after month after year. Each lie is carefully designed to wear us down little by little.

Guard Your "Eye Gate"

We cannot take the Holy Spirit for granted and assume that He will move through dirty vessels. Many times we think we get away with watching sex, violence and profanity on television or at the movies, but the Holy Spirit is right there with us, telling us He is being offended. We are not filled with the Holy Spirit only when we witness to the lost; we are modern-day Arks of the Covenant wherever we go, all the time.

A number of years ago, when our ministry team was in the Midwest, a couple took one of my actresses named

Naomi and me to a movie. After five minutes, I began to "see" something in the Spirit: Demons were coming out of the screen and filling the theater. I realized that I should leave, but I was looking forward to a relaxing time, since it was my first night out after holding meetings all week. Besides, wouldn't it offend our hosts?

I was wrestling with all of this because the Lord kept telling me to leave. He told me that I would be ministering to His people the next day, and He wanted me to be clean. He did not want me to watch that movie.

I had no recourse. It was not okay for me to get slimy at the show when He had told me to leave. I could not become covered with all kinds of filth, and then say, "Forgive me, God. Amen." I would not have been a fit vessel for Jesus in the meetings if I had stayed.

I leaned over to Naomi and said, "Do you see anything coming out of the screen?"

She said, "Oh, no, Jill. You mean we have to leave?"

I whispered that we would be in trouble if we stayed. We both knew it would not be worth it.

I explained to our hosts that the Lord was not allowing us to sit through the movie since there was sex and violence going on. They said, "Well, we have paid our money. If you want to wait in the lobby, that's fine."

Naomi and I plopped on benches in the lobby for the next hour and a half. The best part was that God moved powerfully the next day in both of the services. I knew in my heart that I was clean before the Lord and obedient to what He wanted.

Because I am an artist and I was born and raised in Hollywood, movies have been a way for me to relax and have fun; there are great films out there, and I have a real passion for the movie industry. But the content of many has become perverted, violent and subtly laced with the occult.

We fight many battles in spiritual warfare, and one of the most powerful weapons of the enemy against us is his ability to pollute our minds through the "eye gate." The more evil that passes through our eyes into our hearts and minds, the more clouded our vision becomes and the less we are able to see in the realm of the Spirit.

This infiltration has increased in every aspect of the electronic age—television, movies, the Internet, radio, computer and video games, cartoons. The written word—magazines, books, newspapers, ads, comic books—is also affected. We are, in fact, bombarded by destructive visual images. The danger is that we become culturally desensitized; those images begin to seem normal because they are so familiar. The line between biblical truth and cultural acceptance becomes fuzzy after a while.

Think about it: Are you asking the Lord to help you see in the Spirit realm, but then going to a movie where all kinds of perversion are displayed? Maybe you are attending a meeting where the presence and power of God is moving and you are learning to hear His voice; your child is sitting next to you reading a Harry Potter book, beguiling stories from the second heaven—the satanic realms. Both are supernatural gates.

The enemy has anesthetized us, and we do not even recognize the compromise in our own lives. We need discernment and wisdom desperately. We must be watchful and let the Holy Spirit speak to us about what to do and what not to do. In addition, it is important that we humble ourselves and repent where we have sinned. Before you have the authority to bring freedom to others, you *must* deal with those sins in your own life.

While I am on the subject of entertainment, I want to mention something that I hope will help cast a vision for the arts and media: We must not throw entertainment from the electronic age out the window entirely! We need to wake up to the potential before us. These methods of communication are going to be used powerfully by the Lord to harvest whole nations. We need to be on the cutting edge. This is one of the most strategic battlefronts we face, because it affects the minds, hearts and passions of the masses.

I love the Internet! It is a platform that touches the world. Limitations in ministry are no longer an issue—no one is held back because of education, nationality, age, finances or anything else. Boundless opportunities are at our fingertips in all areas of electronic communication and the arts. But as it stands now, we have lost control of one of the most influential forms of evangelism in the 21st century. We need to repent, take back the territory we have lost and infiltrate all of these ranks for Jesus.

We must become culturally relevant with first-class performances in all of these areas to have an impact on the world. Jesus moves with excellence, and He wants to draw the world back to Himself using the very best plays, movies, music and dance. Remember: Jesus was a master storyteller. The Bible is full of parables, prophecies and truths that are not evident at first glance but that penetrate the heart.

I feel that God wants to give fresh revelation for electronic communication and the arts. We must pray that God will give us brilliant ideas, creative imaginations and funds for these extraordinary means of spreading the Gospel.

Ask for Prophetic Insight

Jesus wants us to go into the war room and get weapons for the new battles we will go up against each day (see Jeremiah 33:3). As Oswald Chambers said: "Prayer does not fit us for the greater work; prayer is the greater work."

During the Gulf War, I kept seeing the same battle scenes on television. I started to get frustrated and said, "Lord, I don't want just news reports. I want to see what is happening in the heavens over the Middle East. What is on Your heart? What are You doing in the realm of the Spirit?"

On Sunday morning our pastor asked our congregation to stand and pray for Israel. The next sound I heard was the audible voice of the Lord: *Michael.*

I asked, "Michael who?"

He said, *Michael the archangel.*

Instantly I had a vision of Michael fighting over Israel. As I asked the Lord what he was doing, I saw that he was in a fierce battle with the prince of Persia.

The Lord continued, *The prince of Persia is trying to pre-empt My timetable, so I have released Michael. The war will end in three days.*

The Lord spoke again and said, *Gabriel.*

I then saw the angel Gabriel moving families and individuals out of harm's way.

The next night I met a pastor from Israel. As I shook his hand I said, "I saw Michael over Israel last night. The war is going to end on the third day." He was interested, and told me that Michael is the archangel over Israel.

The war did end in three days as the Lord had told me.

Ask the Lord strategic questions about your life, family, work, school, city and world events. When He reveals His plan, pray for it to happen just as He said.

Ask for Fuller Understanding

The Lord has taught me to ask Him for language. In other words, I might get part of a picture but not have the words to interpret it for the person it is meant for. How do you explain the mysteries and revelations of the heavens? I always ask the Lord to give me language to describe what He shows me.

Early in my ministry I hardly had language for anything. I can remember praying for a young woman, twenty years old. At the end of the meeting, I laid my hands on her and she screamed bloody murder. The next thing I knew, men's and women's voices were arguing and speaking out of her abdomen. I asked the pastor to come over and we prayed for her. She got quiet, and we felt she had gotten some relief.

Several months later the pastor called and told me that the young woman was dying of cancer of the uterus. She wanted to meet with me. At a restaurant over lunch she said casually, "You know, when my pastor begins to preach, there is something inside of me that just hates him."

I put down my burger and said, "I rebuke that." She turned green and was about to throw up. I said, "And don't you throw up, either!"

I invited her back to my house to stay for a few days, and my four roommates and I prayed and fasted for her. Whenever I cursed the cancer, she screamed. Finally, the Lord said, *Ask her about the little men that are around her.*

I had seen them. They were demons that looked like ugly little men, and they were tormenting her. After her initial shock that I knew about them, she replied, "When I was a little girl about four years old, my father and mother divorced. My father kidnapped me and took me to another state. The woman he married was a witch, and she would curse me. Every night my father would rape me. These little men would appear right before he would come in. They told me they would protect me."

We did not understand in the early days how deliverance was connected to the deep healing of heart issues. But when I asked the Lord to give me greater understanding, He told me that she needed to forgive her father. I told her that if she could forgive, it would break the power of those "little men," or demons. Jesus wanted to be the one to protect her. She got angry and said that she absolutely would not forgive her father. After a lot more discussion, she left.

Later I heard from the pastor that she continued to refuse to forgive her father and had left the church.

I felt tremendous grief because here was a woman dying of cancer and the Lord was giving me insights, but she was not willing to pray them through. Still, I learned from this experience that the Lord would give me the language and information to help me pray specifically.

Remember Your History

We need to look back and remember where we came from. What are our memorial stones? Where has God taken us from? What is our history in God?

Sometimes I am dealing with such heavy warfare that all I can do is lean into His chest and let Him put His loving arms around me. And He says, *It's all right; we have history together. I'm carrying you. It's all right even when you are too tired to pray. I love you and you love Me. I'll hold you. Just cling to My heart.*

He has shown me that it is not how many hours I pray, fast and read the Word, or how well I do all of the disciplines of my spiritual life. It is not just *doing*; it is *being* in His presence. It is an abiding relationship all day long. It is trusting and remembering in the midst of the storms.

God goes into the depths and says, *It's all right. Even in the dark night of the storm when you are at the cross, I'm holding you. Remember that I love you. Remember how I have carried you. Remember that I really like how I made you.*

Because we have a history together, I know that His faithfulness will see me through.

Listen for Prompting

Hearing the voice of the Lord is not just for ministers who speak from a platform. Hearing His voice is a survival mechanism for all of His soldiers. The Lord promises that we will hear His voice and follow after Him (see John 10:4). We can press into Him with the confidence that He desires to speak words of deliverance to us.

Here is an example of what I mean. A friend of mine was hurrying to get home. She ran up to the front door with two bags of groceries. But as she started to open the front door, she paused. She knew that she had locked the door; it was not locked.

She said, "Lord, should I go in or not?"

He said, *No.* So she shut the door quietly, put the bags down, got in her car, went to a phone booth and called the police. They met her at the house. Inside the house they found a known murderer and rapist. She had simply trusted the prompting of the Lord.

God wants us to trust His prompting, the leading of His Holy Spirit. Many times people ask me how I could go alone to all the places I travel. I tell them that I am not alone, but I have to listen closely and trust the prompting of the Holy Spirit. I have to follow Him. If He says, *Stop,* then I have to stop.

Debrief with God

Many times while I am driving home after ministering in a meeting, the Lord will talk to me and teach me. He will say, *Now, you went this direction, but there were three or four other choices. What you did was good, but this would have been better.* Sometimes I make mistakes, repent and He tells me, *That's okay. There's always tomorrow. We will keep trying and learning.*

Even if we do not minister in a meeting, we can still debrief every day about what we experience. Whom did we come in contact with today? We can tell the Lord what we saw and felt and allow Him to speak back to us. Many times He will ask if we noticed such and such. In this way He fine-tunes our spirits to His Spirit.

Go "On Assignment" at Church

Your local church service is an excellent place to fine-tune your skills. Try this assignment at your next meeting.

Begin by telling the Lord you are listening. Ask Him what is happening in church that day. Ask Him how He is going to speak to you and to the people. What will He be initiating?

During worship, pay attention to the stirring of the Holy Spirit. Does He rest on people during the first song, or do you find that His presence does not come until the third or fourth song? Do you sense the Holy Spirit hovering over the room but not settling? Are the people's hearts not melting under His presence and anointing?

Many times in a worship service the room is cold and the presence of God never comes. When that happens, we move into spiritual warfare, asking God to expose obstacles and ambushes. Those who are mature in the Lord, who have character and integrity, do not come to church just to be an audience. They come as participants, as warriors and as watchmen. Even though they are worshiping, they are looking around the sanctuary, praying in the Spirit and asking God what strongholds need to be broken to bring the presence of the Lord down to the people.

During the message, we can look at all the different ways the Holy Spirit is leading the speaker. God uses each person differently. The Holy Spirit might quicken something in your mind that He wants you to pray for the speaker. Even though we are receiving, we are also interceding.

At the altar call, is it time for you to go up and get prayer? Or is it someone else's turn to receive? If so, then it is time to intercede even more fervently. How is the Holy Spirit moving? Is the focus salvation, deliverance, healing of broken hearts?

Every service is different. Every congregation is different. It is never the same and never boring. We could hear the same sermon a hundred times and it would not matter because the Holy Spirit makes it fresh and alive.

Advanced Weapons

The next three topics describe briefly the most powerful weapons in every warrior's arsenal. These are familiar, but I want to mention them because we must understand and use them in order to survive the battles of life. We face evil powers of darkness that want to kill us, but our weapons are fashioned by God Himself, so the enemy is powerless when we activate them.

There are many battle-weary saints and needless casualties because we do not understand that we are really in a war and that Satan truly wants to destroy us. We do not understand our authority over the enemy or the weapons that defeat him.

When we believe the truth of the Word *and* practice it with faith and authority, the enemy will lose significant ground in our lives. But beware: He may retreat for a bit only to come back with a vengeance. The battles will strengthen us, however, and put the enemy in his rightful place—under our feet.

The Mystery of the Cross

The Lord had a secret weapon to save fallen humanity: the power of the cross. Why do I call it a secret weapon? Because it was a plan that only the Father, the Son and the Holy Spirit knew about. The angels did not even know.

The demons certainly did not know when they crucified the spotless Lamb of God that a mystery was about to unfold. They were insane with joy because they thought they had finally won when Jesus was nailed to the cross. But the countdown had begun, and the bombshell was just the opposite of what they expected.

Jesus suffered death and was buried, but on the third day He rose from the dead, defeating death with resurrection power—the most incredible power demonstration in all of eternity. The veil in the Temple was torn in two, and we were allowed entry into the glory and into the presence of Jesus.

Jesus' shed blood on the cross, then, is the doorway to the presence and the anointing of the Lord. It is not just a matter of power; the occult can move in power. We want power through the presence of the man Christ Jesus. We unlock mysteries in the heavens by revelation of Jesus' sacrifice on the cross. As soon as we speak of the blood, the heavens open and the angels and glory come.

The blood of Jesus is full of passion. Out of the wounds come miracles and healing. Out of the blood of the piercings come mysteries and revelations of His great love for His Bride.

The Authority of the Name of Jesus

"You believe that God is one; you do well. So do the demons believe and shudder [in terror and horror such as make a man's hair stand on end and contract the surface of his skin]!

James 2:19, AMPLIFIED

At the name of Jesus, every knee will bow. Every demon of hell and the devil himself are subject to Jesus' powerful name (see Romans 14:11). His name is extraordinary! His name is powerful! His name is spectacular! His name is greater than cancer, greater than divorce, greater than terrorism, greater than financial woes, greater than mental illness, greater than anything we can name. He brings divine reversals by the power and authority of His name.

The Power of the Word of God

For the word of God is living and powerful, and sharper than any two-edged sword, piercing even to the division of soul and spirit, and of joints and marrow, and is a discerner of the thoughts and intents of the heart.

Hebrews 4:12

The declarations of the Word of God can be used like a hammer to pound every stronghold into dust. The Word is also a lethal two-edged sword of the Lord that cuts to the core of the soul and the spirit—and defeats the enemies of the cross in one fell swoop.

Every soldier equips himself before going into battle. He would be an easy target if he were not prepared before the fighting started. How much more should we put on the full armor of God every single day so we are prepared ahead of time to face the battles that will come against us!

Seek the Kingdom first, take your authority, submit yourself to God, resist the devil, cover yourself with the blood of Jesus, declare His promises in the Word and be prepared before you face your day.

The battle is the Lord's, but He has chosen to involve us so we learn, grow and become strong warriors in His army.

Part Four

YOUR
COMMISSIONING

For the word of God is living and powerful, and sharper than any two-edged sword, piercing even to the division of soul and spirit, and of joints and marrow, and is a discerner of the thoughts and intents of the heart.

Hebrews 4:12

10

The Sword of the Lord

There is movement in the heavens to equip God's people. The angels of war are gathering with the resurrection power of the Lamb. It is time to take our places.

In this new battle, warriors will fight with new weapons. God is calling intercessors to go up into the war rooms of heaven and ask Him for armor. We can then look at the territory around us and ask Him how to use our weapons to bring down the strongholds and bring in the glory of the Lamb.

Dreamers and lovers are both warriors, but they hold the sword differently. Revolutionary dreamers and lovers receive fresh vision and revelation for their battles, which involve both justice and mercy. In other words, the Kingdom of God is taken with passionate violence by extreme lovers of the Lord who have the innocence of children! It is a creative strategy for delivering men and women and helping them see their destinies.

Over the last several decades, we have mostly received prophetic words from the Lord for edification and encouragement, not conviction. The Lord is releasing a new season today, however. His words have more to do with the fear of the Lord. A sense of awe and holiness of God is accelerating. It is changing because we are in a time of war.

We need to cry out for open heavens and visitations giving new marching orders for such a time as this. Officers in the Lord's armies are being called forth to legislate—to enact the laws they hear from the councils of God—as heaven invades earth.

I want to share with you an experience that helped me understand this.

A Heavenly Visitation

Recently I was leading a Master Potter conference, and Paul Keith Davis, one of my speakers, was ministering when a corporate realm of glory came into the room. He quoted Matthew 10:41 to the audience: "'He who receives a prophet . . . shall receive a prophet's reward.' You have received many prophets during this conference, and so now you can ask the Lord for a reward. What will you ask Him?"

As I was listening, I began to think about what I would ask Him for. *Lord, what would I ask of You? What do I want?*

I knew the answer. *I want to kiss Your heart, Lord. I want to hear what You hear. I want to feel what You feel. I want to see what You see. I want to know You more. I don't want a name or fame or a title, I just want You! That is what I want.*

At the end of the ministry time, I went up to the podium to say a few things and close the meeting. As Paul handed me the microphone, he said, "Oh, Jill, by the way, there is a huge angel on the side of the stage. He would like to commission you. If you would like to go up there, that would be fine."

I handed the microphone back to him and said, "No problem. I would love to." I went to the side of the stage, seeing and feeling nothing. I kept walking by faith. Suddenly I was thrown violently to the floor.

As I landed I looked up and saw a huge angel, thirty or forty feet tall, glowing with light. A huge sword was piercing my heart; I was pinned to the ground. I knew by revelation that it was an angel of glory, an ancient angel of counsel and might. I was absolutely astounded.

A realm of heaven began to engulf me. It was like liquid fire. I could not move. I could feel the burning through my whole body. I began to tremble. I looked up at his face and saw intensity and raging holiness along with love, but I felt no fear. When I was finally able to get up, I felt like a little child compared to the enormous size of the warring angel.

I put my hands around the handle of the gigantic sword. The angel of the Lord was standing behind me. His strong arms were around me, and his hands covered my hands. He was helping me hold the gigantic, holy sword of the Lord. Lightning was shooting off from it. I looked around and into eternity. A smoky realm of glory was moving all around us.

I knew that no human being could hold this sword by himself. It could be held only with the Lord's help. I could hear the Lord saying, *The Word of the Lord! The Word of the Lord is living and powerful!*

Words paraphrased from Scripture came to me: *The Word of the Lord is living and powerful and is sharper than a two-edged sword. It pierces the soul and the spirit and it divides the joints and the marrow. It discerns the thoughts and the intents of the heart.*

The sword was like the living Word—full of authority. As I held it, the fear of the Lord and the holiness of the eternal One radiated throughout my being. The gigantic ancient angel was still holding the sword with me.

The Lord continued speaking: *It is a sharp sword—it is a sword of war. But it is also a sword of love. It is My raging love. This sword of My love will pierce the hearts of men and women so that they can come to Me.*

I felt a sense of partnership, even union, between the Lord and myself. Then I was whisked under the great expanse of the angel's wings, and we were moving.

Deeper Realms of Eternity

We began soaring above cities and nations. Then, quick as lightning, we were gliding through the heavens. Always around us was the smoky, thick blanket of glory. It seemed to cover the great expanse. The smoke came from incense and the fragrance of God.

We continued moving and I saw fire raging all around us. It seemed as if I was burning with fire, which I took to be the tangible glory of God. I was trembling and shaking.

I could feel that this angel bore the authority of heaven. He actually carried the weight of government. I also continued to sense his fierce love. His face kept changing from the face of a lion to the face of a lamb. I felt he was a guardian of the glory to protect the Lord's name and His fame. In his hand he carried a gigantic sword.

In my hand, still under his wing, I also held a sword and a rod. The Lord revealed to me that this was the priestly sword of Zadok (see Ezekiel 44:15–31) and He was offering it to the Body of Christ. He said: *I am calling the Bride to be like a Zadok priest, a priest of holiness. I am calling you to stand before Me and minister in this place of holiness. A holy priesthood is a higher place of maturity. I am calling My Bride to a place of holiness and fierce love. But it takes greater gifting and deeper intimacy to hold the living sword.*

I looked out into the expanse in front of us, and as far as my eyes could see were legions upon legions of warring angels. They were waiting for the Captain of the Host, the Lord Jesus, to give the word.

Then I realized that in front of me the battle of all battles was forming: Armageddon. This was not just a war between men. This was a war between the fierce angelic hosts and the evil principalities and powers.

These ancient angels of the Lord, the holy army of God, were enormous and fearful to behold. It was as if they were continental angels, global angels. Glory was radiating from them. There was a certain grandness about them, and a feeling of the awe of God surrounded them. They were dressed in military attire—warriors of violence and yet love.

Some had been released and were moving on the earth with special assignments. Others were waiting for orders. I could feel their determination to bring forth the Kingdom of God. Their faces were set like flint. They knew they were part of the end time battle of the Lord. As they looked from the realm of eternity into earth, they moved with grandeur and magnificence to fulfill various assignments.

A Call to War

Then I saw the Captain of the Host, the Lord Jesus Christ. Whenever He spoke, another angelic legion would rumble and move. I could hear the sounds of their chariot wheels and the hooves of horses. I could also hear the sound of a shofar. And the Lord was saying: *I am coming as King. I will release kingly anointing. I will bring justice and judgment—and holiness as never before.*

Then I saw other angelic hosts and chariots of fire waiting for their time to be released. The Lord said: *I am calling you, Jill, and many others as radical forerunners. I am calling you to be end time voices.* I saw the forerunners being sent to cities and nations and standing before presidents and dictators in nothing less than suicidal assignments. I also saw us sharing the Word of the Lord with the poor.

As I looked at the earth, I saw doors opening into different cities, then palaces and embassies. The army of forerunners moved forward with a great show of strength and military prowess. It was more like guerrilla warfare with secret assignments in every arena of influence.

I understood that many of us will be moving in difficult operations within enemy-controlled territories. Sometimes we will be visible but sometimes we will be hidden. The battle will go underground and include incredible assignments to take out top principalities and powers over regions. We will go in like end time secret agents to wreak havoc on the demonic realm.

Then I heard the Lord speak to me. He said: *You are part of a company of forerunners—end time messengers speaking the Word of the Lord. Sometimes you will be visible and will walk into governmental places. But other times you will move in a realm of invisibility and will shift and move things through intercession and apostolic authority. I am releasing my end time generals.*

Yes, evil alliances are being formed, but I am releasing holy alliances. Do not fear. I am releasing warring angels to protect you on these assignments. You will overcome by the blood of the Lamb and by the word of your testimony. You will not love your life even unto death. Even though many are called to martyrdom, not one life will be touched until the hour and the day of the appointment. I am releasing warring angels, guard angels. So do not fear, for every day of your life is ordained.

I am calling My people to be the voice of the Bridegroom, the voice of radical, raging love—for the Kingdom of God is taken with violent love. I am calling you into strategic battle to bring the fear of the Lord, to divide the holy and the profane, to move strategically for My purposes. I will take you places where you will hear demonic plans being made. You will pray and break the power of those plans. You will draw from the armory of the Lord.

I am calling you to bring justice—justice against disease, justice against abuse and bondage. I am calling you to go forth with My heart of love to set the captives free.

How It Changed My Life

This sobering and life-changing visitation was the first of a three-part encounter. It started with the sword of the Lord piercing my heart and ended with my experience of going into the deep chambers of His heart, which I shared in chapter 5. (My CD, entitled *Visitations Vol. 1: The Epic of God's Heart*, gives the full visitation.)

This encounter was not something I could ever have planned. It was a sovereign "break-in" of God in response to the cry of my heart. I wanted to kiss His heart and to be more in love with Him. Even though I was hosting a Master Potter conference at the time, which is a rewarding and fulfilling experience, I still felt exhausted and spiritually bankrupt.

The thing that imprinted my spirit the most about this divine ambush was the depth of His love for each one of us. His fiery, burning heart of love consumed me; I was completely undone! It ushered me into a journey of love in which my heart was awakened and tenderized by Him as never before. For me, this divine ambush was like an "upgrade" in the Spirit to add to my history in God; a transition time; a "garment change"; a season of promotion in the Spirit.

Another thing that had a huge impact on me was the fact that He gave me that dangerous sword and yet said that love was paramount in using it. I felt His jealous love and the urgency of the hour to go outside the walls of the Church and into the dark places to bring back His Bride. It is about the harvest!

I could see that He really is a lovesick Bridegroom and that He will war against everything that hinders love. He will fight for us because He champions us. His strategy is to release the sword of the Lord into the hands of the saints to destroy the enemies of the cross and set the captives free.

Once again the time frames overlap. This preparation for war affects not only future events but everything right now. The world is on the brink of global war. I felt commissioned by the Lord to blow the trumpet and sound the alarm, to be a voice to mobilize the troops to prepare. I felt urgency about the times and seasons we are living in.

At the same time, I experienced a shaking in my own personal life with deeper fires so I would be able to hold more of His glory. It is the paradox of the agony and the ecstasy; the glory and the gore; the mountaintop encounters and heavy spiritual warfare, all colliding with this interactive personal God.

Even though this visitation was a "Kairos moment" in my walk with God, I still have to live an authentic life day after day. God wants us to be supernaturally natural. I often find myself reliving and pondering this precious mystery, which will continue to unfold over the years as the Lord gives more revelation.

How have I used this sword in everyday life? By following the heart of the King—loving the way He loves, seeing with His eyes and hearing what He is saying. Sometimes the Lord has asked me to use the sword to bring promotion in people's situations, ministries or businesses. Other times He has asked me to expose or reveal situations that are cloaked in darkness and deception, as His sword cuts between the precious and the profane. My heart is to activate, equip, mobilize and commission the generations to move in the demonstrations and power of the Holy Spirit to advance the Kingdom of God.

The reality is that you and I are living in the natural world and open to the "suddenlies" of the supernatural breaking in at any time. God is going to use all of us who are willing in this hour.

11

The Final Challenge

My heart's cry is for us to become carriers of the glory. I feel that God wants us to be living flames of fire, radical warriors on the cutting edge of battle strategies. Every place our feet and hands go, we bring the Lord Jesus Christ, the power of resurrection.

Just as the enemy is building a strategy of darkness, so the King of glory is going to release more of His power, presence and life inside of us to defeat it. You know that little song, "This Little Light of Mine"? I hate it. It is not even scriptural. As if Satan could blow out the consuming, unquenchable, holy fire of Christ's presence in us! We are full of the fire of God: "We have this treasure in earthen vessels, that the excellence of the power may be of God and not of us" (2 Corinthians 4:7). We are fragile clay but the glory, the treasure in us, is the Lord. We are weak vessels and yet the fire of God resides in us. What mystery! What destiny!

How much fire is radiating from your life? Are you a thousand-watt bulb? A fifty-thousand-watt bulb? Maybe you are a nuclear reactor with the burning heart of Jesus, bringing light into the darkness of your neighborhood or city.

The Kingdom of God can invade the dominion of Satan only when we are endued with power from on high. We must have spiritual power to advance the Kingdom.

Fire from Heaven

Before Jesus ascended to heaven, He told the disciples to wait and receive the power of the Holy Spirit: "Behold, I send the Promise of My Father upon you; but tarry in the city of Jerusalem until you are endued with power from on high" (Luke 24:49). As they met in the Upper Room, their only agenda was to pray and wait on God. They knew that they needed more. They were not leaving with anything less.

When the Holy Spirit invaded the Upper Room, He established the Kingdom of God on earth. When the glory fell on them, the followers poured out of the house as if drunk on new wine, speaking in the languages of men "from every nation under heaven" (Acts 2:5). The people of the city, amazed and looking for the only plausible explanation they could think of for this outburst at nine in the morning, thought the joyous revelry was drunkenness.

Peter spoke to the people. What do you think an apostle would say as he was experiencing the most awesome revival in history?

He said, "These men are not drunk as they seem." Then as the crowd was laughing in amazement at hearing the wonderful works of God spoken in their native tongues, Peter pierced their hearts with these words of truth: "God has made this Jesus, whom you crucified, both Lord and

Christ" (Acts 2:36). The wind and fire of the Spirit drew a huge crowd that day who heard Peter preach his first sermon. This holy tornado of the Spirit yielded three thousand souls. For the first time, Peter was endued with power and moved in apostolic authority with the power of the Holy Spirit backing his words.

The Church, with her Great Commission for souls, was born that day. If we were God, we probably would not have had the Holy Spirit come that way. But the Lord does things differently. Signs and wonders followed the apostles. Converts came to Jesus, and churches spread like wildfire (see Acts 2:41–47).

Resurrection Power

Acts 5:12–16 says that those early believers brought the sick out into the streets on beds and couches so that perhaps Peter's shadow would fall on them. This disciple carried so much authority, so much of the resurrection power of God, that wherever his *shadow* fell, people were healed and delivered instantly.

Is *your* shadow dangerous? Have you ever prayed for it to be? Just like Peter, you are an earthenware vessel in whom Jesus lives by the power of His Holy Spirit. It is His glorious light in you that casts the shadow. The more of Him that you seek, the more light you will have and the more dramatic your shadow will be.

Would you like for people in your everyday life to be healed and delivered because so much of the resurrection power operates through you? When you walk into a room, a restaurant or a bus station, would you like to walk in as a flame of fire? Would you like for no one to be "safe" in your company because the Lord breaks in suddenly with deliverance and healing? Would you like to change the atmosphere wherever you go because the presence of Jesus around you confronts the darkness? Would you like to have people in your neighborhood knocking on your door for you to pray for them? Would you like to have ambulances parked outside your house because people hear that the miracle power of Jesus is happening there?

Let's take it a step further. Would you like to have hearses parked outside your house as Jesus raises people from the dead? Even if they have been embalmed, God can give them blood. Jesus healed the sick and raised the dead, and He also said, "*Greater* works will you do" (see John 14:12).

Our whole way of thinking has to change because we think too small. Suppose you are part of a prayer team for a city crusade with fifty thousand people in the stadium. How are you going to pray for everyone? Perhaps you are used to praying one-on-one with people at the church altar, but that will not work with the masses. We need the gift of faith to believe for the sovereignty of heaven and a break-in of the Glorious Intruder. Can you believe for the glory cloud of God to have an impact on the entire crowd? That is what is coming!

When heaven touches earth, signs and wonders break out. People start coming out of wheelchairs and running all over the place. Those with no eyes have eyes formed, and they can see for the first time. Others begin to hear. People with skeletal diseases, those crippled and deformed, hear the crunching of bones as body parts knit together. People with cancer, AIDS and all kinds of sicknesses are healed. Others are set free from torment, mental illness and spirits of death. It is not just power; it is resurrection anointing that was won for us on the cross by the power of the blood and set free on earth by the power of the Spirit.

It is the presence of God that fills us with joy and gives us boldness to be living witnesses. As we go out into the marketplace full of the power of God, signs and wonders will follow. God wants to change our thinking. He wants to get us out of religious boxes. He wants us to know that where we walk, He walks in us and around us. Jesus' resurrection power operates through us.

Today the Lord is calling for another Pentecost. I believe that another "Great Awakening" of the Spirit is on the horizon. Imagine the power of Acts combined synergistically with the astonishing signs and wonders of the Exodus. As we approach the Second Coming of Christ, God is going to cause an explosion of power such as we have never seen before.

During these end times, the Holy Spirit will pour out various spiritual gifts of prophecy, healing, discernment, words of knowledge and deliverance. This, in turn, will transform secular society and bring multitudes to the glorious Son. The Gospel will touch every tribe and tongue. We will watch as houses of prayer sprout up across the earth. The Lord is calling a prayer army of holy revolutionaries.

It is a time of horrendous fear versus extraordinary faith—evil alliances versus holy covenants. And the battle of the ages will boil down to two governments colliding—those of God and Satan. Both are after the souls of men—the passion of their hearts. It is passion versus passion, fire versus fire.

As watchmen, we are positioned on the walls to bring down revelation from heaven and shift laws that are cloaked in evil. Whenever there is heavy warfare, God raises up a standard—and calls warriors to their knees.

Apostolic Authority

One of God's names in the Bible is the "Breaker" (see 2 Chronicles 14:11–13; Micah 2:13). A breaker anointing is a catalytic deposit of the Holy Spirit where eternity enters

YOUR COMMISSIONING

the natural realm. It is a holy invasion where the gates of heaven are opened.

This type of anointing breaks through every obstacle and hindrance to the furtherance of the Gospel. It shakes loose every shackle that holds the Church and individuals from coming into their destinies. The breaker anointing is the core anointing for advancement of the apostolic Church.

Today we face tremendous warfare at the gates of our cities. Demonic forces often try to contest the entryway of God's presence. In a service, for example, you may feel tangible heaviness—a "ceiling" blocking your prayers—or oppression. It takes a breaker anointing to open the spiritual atmosphere so heaven can invade earth.

When the breaker anointing comes, it means that individuals, churches, sociopolitical structures and belief systems are revolutionized. This anointing is imperative if we are to see the transformation of our cities.

We must realize, though, that being filled with the Spirit does not "ensure" apostolic power. This power is not operating if conviction does not pierce hearts. Thus we must ask ourselves: Is there fire on the altars of our lives? Only God can make us radical men and women, fathers and mothers who call forth the next generation and birth revival.

Do you want a breaker anointing? Do you want the fullness of the Holy Spirit? The Lord wants to manifest Himself as the Breaker. Get ready! Cry out for this anointing, and contend at your city gates to bring heaven to earth.

The Elijah Anointing

We looked a moment ago at how the fire of God fell and birthed the Church. A forerunner of Pentecost was Elijah, a prophet of fire. He helps us understand our final challenge of confronting the evil in this hour with the *dunamis* power of the Holy Spirit.

178

People often ask about the anointing of Elijah—the desire to have an impact on society and help shift nations governmentally. The reality that the world is an increasingly dangerous place gets more apparent every day. We want to know that there is a God who can take care of us in the face of nuclear threats or plagues or widespread terrorism. Otherwise, once we start living in fear, we start compromising in the name of peace.

So when we talk about the spirit of Elijah, or the Elijah anointing, we mean a prophetic anointing that could come in and make a difference. It means moving in God's power to confront demonic strongholds and see the righteousness and the purity of the Lord prevail.

From the Secret Place of Prayer

Elijah lived under the rule of King Ahab, a cruel and wicked king who was married to an even more demonized queen—Jezebel. They were worshiping Baal, promoting sexual perversion and sacrificing children to idols. It was all-out Satanism.

What I love about Elijah's ministry is that it was formed in the secret place of intimacy and prayer. Then a "suddenly" of God ushered him onto the world scene. As a prophet of God and through the word of the Lord, he was brought to the forefront of society and given a global mandate. What was Elijah's mandate? It was to turn the nation of Israel back to her God and turn the hearts of the fathers back to their children.

Does his battleground sound familiar? How many nations are seduced by financial corruption, lawlessness and terrorism? How many import pornography and other sexual perversions? How many societies are shaken by the enemy in every arena—education, government, business, religion? Are we willing to stand for righteousness? Will we stand for the place of God?

179

Because Elijah had stood in the councils of God, he was able to challenge the council of an earthly ruler. It was already done in the Spirit though prayer. When he declared publicly, "There will be no more rain," he had already confronted the evil power and principality working behind Ahab. It is by answering the call to holiness that we stand against wickedness and perversion.

And the same applies to the case of Jezebel. We must have a solid relationship with the Holy Spirit in order to come against a Jezebel spirit.

The spirit of Jezebel is one that comes to destroy the prophets. It starts with an attempt to abort the newborn. If the spirit cannot abort the baby in the womb, then it tries to abort our call and destiny. This is a demonic spirit that strangles life and destiny and calling and birthright. Actually, it is an international principality that devastates nations. It is not male or female; it is a spirit.

What breaks the power of the Jezebel spirit? People who try to come against this spirit and bind it do not realize that this evil principality is defeated only by the resurrection power of the Holy Spirit. Only the Holy Spirit can take out the Jezebel spirit.

Elijah moved in Kingdom power. He stood in his authority and enacted the word of the Lord, legislating governmentally. Not only did Jezebel confront Elijah on Mount Carmel; this evil principality—this Jezebel spirit—confronted the *God* of Elijah. And at Elijah's word, God answered with fire!

When Elijah spoke, God backed him up. This is our test for the Elijah anointing: Do we see any signs and wonders? Do we see anybody healed? Are people hungry to get our wisdom and revelation because we hear from God? Do people come to us because we are messengers of the Lord?

Many people walk in defeat because the enemy has gained legal access to places in their lives through sin, compromise, idolatry, disobedience and addictions. If you have common ground with the enemy, then you cannot confront the darkness around you. You must be clean in those areas yourself. This is a call to holiness! There needs to be something in us that presses into the face of Jesus, no matter what. We say, "Lord, where there are areas of darkness in my life, where there is any compromise or brokenness from unforgiveness, bitterness or cynical attitudes in my life, I want You to bring Your fire of conviction upon the altar of my heart."

The Soldiers Emerge

As God empowers His people, we will find that we are placed strategically in cities and nations. The Lord is setting in place end time soldiers who will emerge and lead the troops to war. We are going to open the gates for the King of glory to come in. He is not going to show up with just a sign here and a wonder there. He is going to establish beachheads as His warriors take hold of our prophetic birthright and welcome revival.

This will be a fresh outpouring of the Lamb of God. It will be as if the doors of a huge warehouse open and the Spirit hands out mantles of anointing, scepters of rule and government, swords to bring justice and keys to open doors for His people.

Jesus is going to send thousands and thousands of people full of His resurrection glory throughout the world. That includes you! You will be full of His presence and full of His power. Your gifts will make room for you to go where He calls you. You will impregnate the atmosphere with Jesus Christ, the Glorious Intruder.

How much do we want Him? How desperate are we? You see, during revival it is as if there is a tear in the heavens and the throne of God comes to earth. When we pray, "Thy Kingdom come, Thy will be done," we are asking that the government of God come to earth. And when the government of God comes to earth, He brings His heart for the lost.

Are you excited? What we are seeing right now looks like a wave far out in the ocean. But it is sweeping forward, and as it gets closer its true height and power will become evident. It is a tidal wave of glory. When that wave crashes onto the shore, people will start falling down on their faces and crying out because our God is moving in our midst.

This is a corporate move, but we also need to realize that the Body is made up of individuals. Each one of us has choices to make. We have to decide whether we will say yes or no, because it could cost us our lives.

The Gospel: Not for Sale

I was ministering recently in an African nation, and one day at a local restaurant the Lord opened the door for me to speak into the life of an influential man. As we sat there, the Lord began to reveal things to me about him. I knew that he was a Muslim, but the Lord also showed me that he was part of the Mafia and dealt powerfully in the black market. Even though he was truly warm and gracious, he had governmental weight on the "dark side" and was the main gatekeeper in the city.

As we talked, I found that I liked him. We really connected. Several other people were at the table with me, and one of them was trying to convert him. A friendly bantering ensued.

Finally, I looked at this man with a heart of compassion and said, "Listen, you can't have my Jesus."

He stared at me for a moment and spoke in total disbelief. "Why not?" he asked.

"Coming to Jesus is not cheap salvation," I explained. "Jesus is not for sale, so you can't have Him." I started to challenge him that it meant a commitment of the heart. He had to be willing to lose everything to gain Jesus. He could not be a Muslim and a Christian at the same time.

"You are known in the Muslim world. In fact you are part of the Mafia."

"Who told you that?"

I reminded him that I had just gotten off the airplane and met him for the first time. I told him that I knew nothing about him, and that the Lord was downloading me with details as I was sitting there. "If you come to Jesus," I continued, "it will be very dangerous. You and your family could lose your lives. You are not just one of the village people at the crusades who can simply come forward and accept the Lord. It will mark you. It could cost you everything. This has to be weighed very carefully because this could be a life-and-death situation."

"I really like you," he said as he looked intently at me and grabbed my hand, "but you scare me!"

"That's good," I said, as he laughed nervously. "Jesus is dangerous."

We had an understanding. I could feel that we respected each other. He was attracted to danger—it was part of his lifestyle—so he was intrigued by my honesty. He liked it that my sword was drawn, so to speak.

We left as friends. I know that the Lord will bring others across his path in the days to come. And I know I will see him again. He strikes me as a Nicodemus who will come to the Lord in secret and help finance the Kingdom.

As the Lord was leading me in wielding the sword of the Lord with this man, my heart was moved with mercy and compassion; but at the same time, the Lord was also drawing a line of demarcation with His justice and truth.

So often we want people to accept Jesus, but there is no conviction, no genuine repentance and no understanding of the cost. The Gospel is not cheap. If we are authentic—and

the world knows if we are—then their lives will be transformed for the Kingdom.

Our Awakened Hearts

The key is love. It is going into the heart of Jesus. We all
want to move in signs and wonders and do great exploits,
but it all starts with His heart of love. As we are awakened
to bigger purposes for our journeys, God can touch our own
hearts at deeper levels. Then we can connect to other people
and we can be deliverers. When we walk in our destinies,
when we dream and love and war in the heavenlies, then
we gain clearer sight of ourselves and others. The more I
understand my destiny as an "eye," the more I can encourage you in your destiny as an "arm" or a "leg."

It is love that keeps us on the journey to our destinies,
embracing the ups and the downs; the joy and the suffering;
the pain and the passion. We celebrate life with all of its
emotions and passions because our hearts are awakened.

When I move in the anointing and see realms of glory
start to open and heaven starts to connect with earth, the
whole atmosphere becomes alive and God is present. It
is the most exciting thing in the world! It is as if eternity
has come.

Then the Holy Spirit stirs hearts. Some people begin
crying, some laughing, some pondering the deep place of
God and wanting more. People are awakened to dream
big dreams, to be fully alive. It is like seeing layers come
off of their minds and hearts when the fire of our creative
God touches them. I live for that. I live for heaven touching earth.

I want you to be so full of this resurrection passion that,
even though you might be going through suffering and loss
and disillusionment, you can still say, "I love the Lord so

much I'm not going to quit. I'm not going to go halfway through my life and say, 'Forget it; it's too tough.'"

No matter what season you are in, remember that we all experience cycles of life as the Lord declares:

> To everything there is a season, a time for every purpose under heaven: A time to be born, and a time to die . . . a time to weep, and a time to laugh; a time to mourn, and a time to dance . . . a time to love, and a time to hate; a time of war, and a time of peace. . . .
> He has made everything beautiful in its time. Also He has put eternity in their hearts.
>
> Ecclesiastes 3:1–2, 4, 8, 11

You can live in the realm of strategies, blueprints, dreams and visions and travel in the heavenly realms of God.

We must stand with each other and declare, "Come on; we're all in this together." When the Kingdom of God comes, we link arms together and keep declaring, "We're going to live and not die. Our hearts will keep expanding to hold the deep things of God."

The Challenge

Dancing with destiny!

Our wild, awesome, holy God has plans for you that are more creative than you could even dare to imagine. If you give yourself to Him, it will be exhilarating. That is the truth. Being alive will take on a totally new meaning when you let go of controlling your life and destiny and let God move creatively with you.

There is something about the words *danger* and *adventure* that resonates in the core of who you were created to be. You love the intrigue of the unknown, and you want to be fully engaged. You hear the call of the wild, the ancient longing of every soul, and you want it. Deep down inside, you *know* that you were created for more than you are presently living.

Don't let regrets gnaw away at your heart. No one can go back and fix what has already been done, but God can restore the years the locusts have eaten (see Joel 2:25). He can redeem every single thing in your life that the enemy used to gain ground.

Please hear me! The Lord wants your life to be as beautiful as it was in His mind when He *first* thought of you. When you were in your mother's womb, He knew you and called you by name. He looked at you and declared proudly, "You are Mine." You were His idea. When you agree with Him—and there is power in agreement—you break the grip of the enemy in your life.

This is very important. If you cannot agree with Jesus that you were "fearfully and wonderfully made," then you are agreeing with Satan's lies that "you are a loser . . . you don't matter . . . you will never change." It is time to break agreement with him about who you are. When you do, your life will change dramatically.

It is never too late to allow God to awaken His dreams for your life. *It is only too late when you have taken your last breath.*

Imagine that Jesus shows you a large beautiful book with your name embossed in gold. It is filled with your destiny—all of the plans and dreams He ever had for you on earth, all your battles and tears, your victories and defeats. As He opens it, your secret history is revealed in the various chapters and seasons of your life. Revelation and glory come off the pages. As you see different names and faces, memories race through your spirit.

Then His gaze shifts to a small thin book, and He says to you, "This is what you have accomplished so far."

Your eyes are drawn back to the large book of what is ahead.

"I have so much more for you!" He says. "Will you go on the high adventures with Me? Will you trust Me?"

Now that you see what God has planned for you—your destiny—you cannot wait to run the race! Your heart burns with new zeal and determination to make your life count for Him. You long to follow Him with everything that is in you. "Catch me if you can!" you shout to those around you.

A Dangerous Prayer

Are you ready to pray one of the most dangerous prayers you may have ever prayed in your life? Perhaps you want to pray this out loud day after day, declaring it with your whole heart. You will see changes happening.

God, tenderize my heart again so that I desire to return to You as my first love. Wherever my heart has drifted or gotten lukewarm, return me back to You. God, I give You permission to do whatever it takes to make me wholly Yours. Set my heart on fire for You. Send a holy ambush of Your Spirit into my life to usher me out of the ruts that have hindered me from being a dreamer, a lover and a warrior.

Please forgive me for [here be as specific as you can be and take as long as you need]. Thank You for Your total forgiveness of my sins. That is such a precious gift to me.

How I ache to know You more! Draw me close and speak tenderly to my heart. I want to develop a secret history with You, Lord. Captivate my heart with the gaze of Your eyes. I want to see You face-to-face and not through the lattice, as Your Word says. Put Your seal on my heart so I am fully Yours.

Now, Lord, I ask You to release the fiery whirlwind of Your presence with a fresh impartation of Your heart into my heart. I ask You to revolutionize my life from the inside out. Let an earthquake in my heart break up the fallow ground. Let the

187

lightning of God strike me so that I become God-conscious instead of self-conscious.

Jesus, I am ready to give up control of my life and put You in charge again. Forgive me for thinking that I know what is best for my life. It is hard for me to let go; the warfare has been so intense and the storms of life so great. But I can see that my way is not working. I am heartsick about my life. I want to run to You and not from You. Give me grace and humility to accept Your timing in my life.

Burn in me a holy desperation and craving for You. I need a profound touch from You, a fresh baptism of fire from the Holy Spirit. I want a force field of Your glory surrounding me so I am dangerous for God. Will You radiate Your love and power through my life so I can do exploits as You promised?

I want to be a carrier of Your glory and go outside the walls of the church, touching people in every arena of life. Lord, I want to know the times and seasons we live in.

Let me see people through Your eyes and not my own; help me feel Your heart for those around me. Break my heart for the lost. Cause revival to burn so deeply in my spirit that others cannot help but be changed by coming in contact with me.

I do not want business as usual, Jesus! I want a radical visitation from You. I must have a visitation. I want an open heaven over my life. Will You help me to legislate Your mandates from heaven, to bring them to earth so I see things from Your perspective and not my own? I am asking You for divine strategies so Your Kingdom will come.

Open my eyes so that I can see what is happening in the realm of the Spirit. How I need keen discernment for the days I live in. I want to get Your plans, Your blueprints, so I do not build on the "land mines" the enemy has planned for me.

I want my heart to bless Your heart and give You the love that You deserve. Awaken my heart to worship You. I want to be one who desires You only.

Lord, I want to give You my life no matter what the cost. Even as You died for me, help me to be willing to die for You.

You are worth everything I have. All I am—my past, present and future—is at the foot of the cross. Take all of me.
   Help me to be a big dreamer with You, dreamer God.
   Help me to be an extravagant lover of You, my Bridegroom.
   Help me to be a fierce warrior for You, my King. Amen.

The Invitation

The atmosphere changes as the perfume of your prayers welcomes heaven into your midst. You begin to hear a glorious celestial choir. Indescribable splendor envelops you.

Suddenly the Bridegroom King stands before you. Flowing from His being are music and messages that transcend time and eternity. Gazing intently into your eyes, He holds you in His glorious embrace. "You are My beloved," He says, "and you always will be." You gaze back into His fiery eyes and feel His unrelenting love bathing you in His consuming devotion.

As He hands you a long-stemmed red rose, you hear Him whisper, "Will you dance with Me?"

Jill Austin, founder and president of Master Potter Ministries, has ministered with a catalytic prophetic anointing for more than 25 years. She has a passion to influence the Body of Christ to return wholeheartedly to first love with Jesus and to experience personal encounters with Him that will awaken their destinies.

With a proven prophetic track record and an exciting biblical perspective, accompanied by signs and wonders, Jill is a popular speaker at conferences worldwide. She is known for her unique friendship with the Holy Spirit and her ability to impart radical hunger for the Lord Jesus Christ. Jill has bridged international, denominational and generational divides on hundreds of ministry trips into Asia, Europe, Africa, Canada and the United States, and ministered to thousands of leaders in the Body of Christ, imparting fresh passion for ministry. Her vision: to see historic revival in which cities and nations are transformed by God's glory.

Ordained by the International Church of the Foursquare Gospel, the International House of Prayer in Kansas City by Mike Bickle and Harvest International Ministry (HIM) in Pasadena by Dr. Ché Ahn, Jill is also a member of the apostolic leadership team of HIM and holds membership in the Founders Circle of the Deborah Company with Dr. Cindy Jacobs.

An award-winning professional potter by trade, Jill has a degree in fine arts from the University of Puget Sound, Tacoma, Washington, and an MA in art education from the

University of Washington in Seattle. She has been featured on *The 700 Club*, PTL, TBN and other television programs, as well as numerous radio shows, and is the author of two prophetic allegories, *Master Potter* and *Master Potter and the Mountain of Fire*. She has published articles in *Charisma*, *Ministries Today*, *Kairos*, *The Voice of the Prophetic* (Elijah List), *Last Days*, *SpiritLed Woman* and many more. She also contributed to the *Women of Destiny Bible*. Jill resides in Southern California.

For more information, or if you would like to have Jill speak at your conference or church, please contact her at:

Master Potter Ministries
25602 Alicia Pkwy, #124
Laguna Hills, CA 92653
(949) 600–8871
www.masterpotter.com
info@masterpotter.com

The two-book series *Master Potter* and *Master Potter and the Mountain of Fire* is a powerful Christian allegory that addresses the current fascination with supernatural phenomena.

 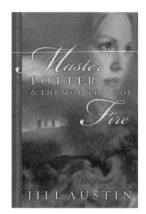

Visitations Vol. 1: The Epic of God's Heart is the first of a unique series of recordings describing personal heavenly visitations.

Jill's powerful teaching CDs can be ordered online at www.masterpotter.com.